Elisabeth Schwarzkopf

Kirsten Liese

Elisabeth Schwarzkopf
From Flower Maiden to Marschallin

With Photographs by Lillian Fayer

𝄞
AMADEUS
PRESS
An Imprint of Hal Leonard Corporation
New York

Amadeus Press
An Imprint of Hal Leonard Corporation
7777 West Bluemound Road
Milwaukee, WI 53213

Trade Book Division Editorial Offices
19 West 21st Street, New York, NY 10010

Published by Amadeus Press in 2009

Originally published by Molden Verlag in 2007

Printed in the United States of America

Arrangement by the literary agent Swantje Steinbrink
Translation and collaboration by Susannah Worth and Charles Scribner III
Editing by Charles Scribner III and Marion Mauthe
Production by Marion Mauthe
Book design by Alexander Schuppich

Library of Congress Cataloging-in-Publication Data is available upon request.

ISBN 978-1-57467-175-9

www.amadeuspress.com

Contents

Foreword

Dietrich Fischer-Dieskau

Elisabeth Schwarzkopf was surely the only true vocal *artist* of the last century. She had the unique ability to lead conscious awareness back to the unconscious mind. I am proud to have been by her side throughout the decades, united by similar aims. She should remain alive in our memories, which I hope this book will do its part to ensure.

Side by Side with Elisabeth Schwarzkopf: An Interview with Lillian Fayer

The first photographic series you made of Elisabeth Schwarzkopf was in 1947. While the bomb-damaged Wiener Staatsoper [Vienna State Opera] was being reconstructed, the legendary Wiener Mozart Ensemble attempted to play in an alternative venue, the Theater an der Wien. What were working conditions like at the time?

I was lucky. Our studio, including our showcases and displays, was situated opposite the opera house—an area now known as Opernringhof—in the part of Heinrichshof which had not been destroyed by bombs. Our technical equipment had survived the bombs without any fire or water damage. The essential materials for making portraits were impossible to get hold of, but my father in America was able to help. After the war ended, I had to use glass sheets to produce the very first portraits, including one of Herbert von Karajan.

Elisabeth Schwarzkopf was quite a perfectionist at that time, influencing decisions about her costumes, hair, and stage makeup. To what extent did she herself direct the photographs?

Elisabeth never took control of the direction—she remained focused on the role! Her perfectionism in this respect was a positive contribution to our working partnership. She was uncomplicated, patient, she

allowed me to do as I wished, and always trusted me, but when choosing the final photographs she was a discerning critic. I would always take two or three different shots of one motif, so that she could choose the best. It was a delight to photograph her.

You were one of the first professional theater photographers in Vienna to make black-and-white autographed postcards of singers and directors. Previously there had only been a demand for such images of Hollywood actors. How did you come to work with the Staatsoper?

The motivation came from the artists who were dissatisfied with the amateurish snapshots which had been in circulation. Most of them knew me already because they had come into the studio for private work and then later recommended me for professional work. It was also a natural continuation of my ongoing work with the Salzburg Festival. From 1952 to 1961 the artists' portraits became famous there, having been widely circulated as autographed cards.

In one photo [p. 32] from your series taken in 1947, Elisabeth Schwarzkopf looks very similar to Marlene Dietrich, who had her molars removed so that the light and shade were elaborately manipulated to give her cheeks a more hollow appearance. What tricks did you use to reveal the particular mystery of the diva Schwarzkopf?

Elisabeth was so beautiful and photogenic that no tricks were needed, and I was careful to light the shots correctly. God graced her with a marvelous facial structure. In contrast, Maria Callas, who was undoubtedly also a beautiful and photogenic woman, had a very low forehead. Though I never photographed Callas myself, I know from colleagues that it was very difficult to conceal her low forehead.

You photographed all the famous singers at the Wiener Staatsoper from the mid–twentieth century, including Irmgard Seefried, Sena Jurinac, Erich Kunz, Paul Schöffler, George London, Otto Edelmann, Dietrich Fischer-Dieskau, Lisa Della Casa, and Anneliese Rothenberger. However, you had a special relationship to Elisabeth Schwarzkopf, so that you abandoned the formal *Sie* and developed a friendship. What did you especially like about her?

Her sincerity, her friendliness, her self-criticism, and the fact that she never put on airs and graces. Admittedly her sincerity made her many enemies, because she always spoke her mind and was by no means always flattering . . .

But it is also true that you were free to offer criticism . . .

It annoyed me that she never wore makeup in her private life, because with her natural pallor—blond hair and light blue eyes—her beauty could not be noticed.

You told her this rather bluntly. How did she react?

She took it to heart, but it struck me that her good intentions to make a change for the better did not last long.

In which role or in which performance did Elisabeth Schwarzkopf impress you the most?

As Elvira in Mozart's Don Giovanni. *At a rehearsal in Salzburg I completely forgot to press the shutter release button because her Elvira aria was so captivating.*

Photographic shoots are often lengthy affairs. How much time did a singer have to set aside for a sitting with you?

It was very different. When a singer came to the studio in costume, the sittings took at least half a day. I also worked in a room at the opera house, which singers usually used for vocal warm-ups before a performance. Usually we only had five minutes for a shoot when we were working at this "studio on the fly." Of course, under these circumstances we were very dependent on the cooperation of the singers. They would come to us during a rehearsal or performance and then scurry straight back to the stage afterwards. Only a single sitter, the baritone Paul Schöffler, made the process last longer because he was an extremely impatient person. As he once again rushed me with cries of "Faster, faster!" I threatened him: "Mr. Meistersinger, when you next perform a monologue on stage I will be there near the stage manager, calling 'Faster, faster!'" Thereafter he no longer rushed me and was willing to set aside the necessary time to help make the best photographs we could.

Your work, however, was not only limited to portraits. You also worked at the rehearsals for premieres, to which the photographers were specifically invited.

At these rehearsals I would race around the entire opera house to work from a variety of standpoints. Although sometimes access was limited or entirely impossible—one could only take limited photographs because some of the costumes were not yet finished or had to be altered.

In Karajan's era I was allowed to go in and out of the opera house to visit all the rehearsals and work unhindered on stage beside the stage manager, even during performances. Thus not only was our archive vastly expanded, but also that of the Staatsoper itself. I was the only one to record on camera Placido Domingo's performance of Don Carlos *in May 1967.*

What kind of relationship do you yourself have with music?

When I was young, I studied singing for a few years, so in this respect I understand a great deal about the voice. And above all, I love music!

Which of the photographs you took of Elisabeth Schwarzkopf do you personally like the most?

It is very difficult to emphasize one individual photograph, for with her ideal facial structure she was absolutely one of the most photogenic singers, which is why you can find so many good photographs of her in the archives. However, if I had to name a favorite photograph, it would be a portrait that is entirely in white [p. 104], in which she looks out mischievously from the picture.

I also think the Capriccio Countess *[p. 97] with the harp is a perfect dream, although the colors border on kitsch for today's taste. But that does not bother me.*

This *Capriccio* Countess was originally taken in subtle orange tones. What did the conversion from black-and-white to color mean for you?

I found it hard to use the first color materials that were available in Austria. Therefore I waited a few years until Kodak came over from America. Kodak had developed a special portrait negative which had very natural colors. One can probably no longer express the same enthusiasm for good colors, because today they are nearly always accurate. Back then it was a sensation.

To what extent was it also a melancholy farewell to the black-and-white aesthetic?

Of course, especially since it turned out that black-and-white creates a more dramatic effect, which is why most photographers return to it.

The last time you met with Elisabeth Schwarzkopf was to choose the photographs for this book.

That was exquisite, as we two old ladies chatted to each other, a little bit mixed up and woolly at times. I enthused about a concert with the Berlin director Christian Thielemann, which was an exceptional experience for the whole Musikvereinssaal, whereupon Elisabeth looked at me as sternly as a teacher and the following dialogue ensued: Elisabeth: "Can you actually read scores?" Me: "No." "Then you cannot be allowed an opinion." "Why?" "Judgments are only permitted to educated specialists who understand something of the subject. You understand nothing about it, so do not judge it!" "If that is so, darling Elisabeth, give me back all the bravos that I have called out to you." "There are already plenty of others."

Kirsten Liese interviewing Lillian Fayer, June 2007.

"Time, it is a strange thing": An Homage

Elisabeth Schwarzkopf *was* the Marschallin: beguilingly beautiful, majestic, noble, and astute. When in Richard Strauss's *Der Rosenkavalier* she reflected upon the past, about growing old, about the loss of her feminine allure, it was always with a hint of melancholy, but never sentimentality. One could easily forget that it was in fact Hugo von Hofmannsthal who wrote those timeless poetic verses. In every performance, Elisabeth Schwarzkopf gave the impression that she felt these emotions anew, as though these thoughts ran through her mind spontaneously. She performed the monologues and the grand concluding trio not just on one occasion but in every performance with detailed precision.

In this, one of her signature roles, Elisabeth Schwarzkopf combined an aristocratic Viennese bearing with breathtaking pianissimo head notes, and she lent an air of refinement to the amorous adventures. One cannot forget how she mischievously drives Baron Ochs crazy when she recommends to him her young lover Octavian (whom Ochs has just seen moments before as Mariandl the chambermaid) as his bridegroom's ambassador. Or how she injects a fatal charm into the words, "*And in the afternoon I will send you a messenger, Quinquin, and leave word whether I shall drive to the Prater.*"

Also unforgettable are her inimitable half-whispered delivery of *Ich weiss auch nix, gar nix*. (I, too, know nothing, nothing at all.) in the moment that she relinquishes her youthful lover in the third act, and her final sigh, "*Ja, ja.*" Her breadth of expression can be described through these few words: kindheartedness, melancholy, pride, and wisdom. Her own analysis was appropriately clear-sighted: "The Marschallin is not a virtuoso role in which you may flaunt yourself. With the Marschallin you must touch your audience." That was the key to her great artistry: Elisabeth Schwarzkopf could move her audience to tears.

It was in the spring of 2005, one and a half years before her death, that I experienced being with Elisabeth Schwarzkopf up close for an entire weekend. On the occasion of her approaching ninetieth birthday, I requested an interview. It was my fifth attempt, but I was hopeful that Elisabeth Schwarzkopf, who had always shown herself to be willing, would fulfill my wish. The first request was during my university exams in 1988, when I wanted to make contact to dedicate a piece on *Der Rosenkavalier* to her. With her first response she did not include the photograph I had requested, but my letter was not in vain; some time later I received just what I wanted: a wonderful portrait of her Marschallin, taken by Lillian Fayer.

My first request for an interview was in 1994, for the Bavarian Radio Network. Elisabeth Schwarzkopf promised to do it at first, but then had to cancel each time owing to health reasons. Who would have dared to hope that my time would finally come when this elderly lady was so close to her ninetieth birthday? What she offered me there at Telfs was so much more than an interview. I was allowed to accompany her all weekend long. I was able to experience her teaching as well as her private self. She organized my accommodation in a romantic little hotel, in the same quarter in which she was staying, picked me up in a taxi to attend the master classes at the Villa Schindler, invited me during the lunch break for coffee at the Mieminger Plateau, in the picturesque heart of the mountains, and in the evening invited me for a glass of wine. On such occasions, when my recording equipment was switched off, more personal details would be revealed. She explained that earlier in life not only were men intoxicated by her beauty but also women, who sometimes stormed her dressing room. I was astounded by her wit and openness when I referred to a production of *Don Giovanni* in Berlin by the agent provocateur Peter Konwitschny, who altered the libretto to represent Anna and Elvira as lesbians in the final act. The *grande dame* was not in the least embarrassed; instead she said with disarming humor, "He probably thought he was supposed to make something comic for the Komische Oper [Comic Opera], don't you think?"

Above all, Elisabeth Schwarzkopf impressed me with her generosity. Unseemly things were said about her, that she was a demanding, mean, bitter old battle-axe. Hardly anyone mentioned that she charged no fee for her master classes, and not a single euro for the private teaching hours at her home. She always bore in mind that singers without constant engagements do not earn much. She repeatedly ensured that the "children," as she lovingly called young talent, should never pay for the hotel where they stayed. She would also give taxi drivers a princely tip.

In addition, even in her old age Elisabeth Schwarzkopf never assumed an air of self-importance. Indeed, she was pleased that long-standing admirers arrived to request her autograph. However, her primary concern was to turn her attention to her students and to support great talent. The fact that she seemed milder during this time was perhaps the effect of the comfortable atmosphere at the small and intimate Villa Schindler. A television crew stood by the door but they were soon sent home, so our meeting retained its intimacy.

Many amusing situations arose. For example, during a master class, when a soprano began an aria from Lehár's operetta *Der Zarewitsch*—"One will come, who will desire me, one will come, to whom I'll belong."—Elisabeth Schwarzkopf broke her off: "It is too chaste. There should be far more pleasant anticipation within the sound. All the men must immediately think, 'Ah, so she's that kind of girl.'" And taking a sideswipe at the shock tactics of contemporary musical theater, she added: "You will, of course, already be stripped naked on stage!"

Certainly there were moments in Telfs when Elisabeth Schwarzkopf became more resolute and unyielding. When someone sang an atrocious note, she would tell them so quite bluntly. At earlier master classes that candor was taken amiss, but her protégés at the Villa Schindler grew to appreciate her meticulous method of polishing and perfecting.

They regarded their instruction for what it was: a great chance to achieve their highest possible potential. On the rare occasion that Elisabeth Schwarzkopf gave a student the thumbs up, that person could be proud, knowing it was high praise indeed.

Sometimes Elisabeth Schwarzkopf also had remarkable suggestions for the piano accompanists. It was not rare for her to recommend a more economical use of the forte pedal. That is all the more noteworthy as Elisabeth Schwarzkopf never concerned herself with historical performance practice; yet amazingly, decades before Nikolaus Harnoncourt, she instinctively preferred the pianist Walter Gieseking, who with stylistic confidence abandoned the forte pedal throughout their joint rehearsal for the recording of Mozart lieder.

I was particularly affected by one moment when the elderly lady, with an almost maternal reassurance, supported her student, who was consistently failing to reach the highest pianissimo notes: "I know that you can do it, otherwise I would not demand it. Only you do not know it. But soon, when you discover it yourself, the audience will be left flabbergasted."

Elisabeth Schwarzkopf not only demanded perfection from her pupils, but also from herself. "Oh, dear, I think we made a lot of mistakes that time," she often said, somewhat comfortingly, if something did not quite come off. Subsequently she still tended to apologize for trifling things that she felt should have been done differently. She was also severely critical of her recordings. She distanced herself artistically from more than a few, and struggled to reconcile herself to all the CD recordings principally because of technical defects in the remastering: "I have a high-quality CD player and the best loudspeakers at home, but when I listen to these recordings, I often do not recognize myself at all."

She felt better represented by the multitude of photographs from which she chose her favorites for this book. Elisabeth Schwarzkopf always had precise ideas for her costumes and stage make-up, and she often did her own makeup. In the star portraits she would smile with her mouth closed over the small but charming gap between her two upper front teeth, and she aptly described herself as an *Augenmensch* (visual person). She was a keen photographer herself and showed great talent, using zoom lenses and experimenting with unfocused images. Her favorite subject was colorful flowerbeds, and she was especially proud of her tulip pictures.

More than anything, Elisabeth Schwarzkopf had a weakness for beautiful photographs, which she hoarded almost obsessively. Her estate included large quantities of many different images. Claire Erlanger, Walter Legge's secretary and one of Elisabeth Schwarzkopf's closest acquaintances, remembers how, even at the age of eighty-nine, in the last years of her life, she continued to order dozens more copies of prints that she already owned. It seemed to be a survival tactic learned from the rationing and deprivation of the Second World War. Like time-lapse photography, the images illustrate all the stages of her life, in which there was no separation between professional and private. Her father, Friedrich Schwarzkopf, whom she affectionately called "Poppi," was a secondary-school master who often sang folk music and awoke in his daughter a love of singing; from her caring, omnipresent mother, Elisabeth, she inherited her discerning, keen, resolute ear. It was her parents who encouraged her from a young age, despite political upheavals and financial hardships, to concentrate solely on her training as a singer.

This education began at age eighteen at the Musikhochschule in Berlin, where Elisabeth Schwarzkopf finally found peace after those turbulent years in the German provinces. Only a few years after her birth in 1915, in Jarotschin near Posen, following the First World War, the Schwarzkopf family moved successively to Liegnitz, Wahlstatt, Magdeburg, and Cottbus, before coming to Berlin. Here she made her debut in 1938 as the second Flower Maiden in Wagner's *Parsifal* at the Deutsches Opernhaus. A photograph of this debut is unfortunately no longer obtainable, but it probably showed her wearing a costume similar to that of the later Undine, one of

around forty roles that she performed in only a few seasons. At the beginning she mostly took on small parts such as the Young Shepherd in *Tannhäuser*, the Taumännchen in *Hänsel und Gretel*, the First Noble Orphan in *Der Rosenkavalier*, and Ida in *Fledermaus*, but naturally also some larger roles, such as Lortzing's Undine, Zerbinetta in *Ariadne auf Naxos*, Musette in *La Bohème*, the Ännchen in *Freischütz*, and Susanna in *The Marriage of Figaro*. The Deutsches Opernhaus was the site of a crucial encounter with the baritone Karl Schmitt-Walter, who referred her to the famous coloratura soprano Maria Ivogün, who helped Elisabeth Schwarzkopf to improve her technique radically and who had an important effect on her later career as a lieder singer. Ivogün's husband, the eminent pianist Michael Raucheisen, accompanied Elisabeth Schwarzkopf at several of these recitals.

It is most fitting that while still a voice student, the young *Augenmensch* Schwarzkopf took part in several films. Although her roles were limited to cameo appearances—as the seductive Carmen in Werner Hochbaum's drama *Drei Unteroffiziere* (1938–39), or as Puccini's dying Mimi in Erich Waschneck's melodrama *Nacht ohne Abschied* (1941–43) opposite the soon-to-be famous tenor Peter Anders—one fact is inescapable: with her sensual, enchanting appearance and her high, light voice the apprentice Schwarzkopf could always hold her own with the female stars of these films.

Her greatest and most noteworthy role was in Bernhard Wentzel's short (twenty-one minute) feature film, *Das Mädchen von Saint Coeur* (1939–40).[1] To be sure, the simple and unremar-

[1] The only known copy of this film is preserved in the Bundesfilmarchiv (Federal Film Archive) in Berlin.

kable screenplay by Werner E. Hintz, together with the far-fetched plot, may account for the fact that this slice of film history attracted little attention and quickly passed into oblivion. It is nonetheless a rare, precious document of Elisabeth Schwarzkopf's beginnings as an opera singer—in which, by the way, she retouched the gap in her teeth—as well as of her theatrical talent.

It tells the story of a young singer from the provinces in Belgium who achieves a meteoric rise to stardom by tricking the director of the Brussels Opera. Henry, the husband of the crafty Thérèse de Lorm, is secretary to the opera director Duval; he arranges his wife's coup by staging an automobile breakdown during a drive with his boss. Everything goes like clockwork. A tire bursts, the car is stuck in the middle of the country road, and suddenly a delightful song wafts from a haystack: a young shepherdess as an undiscovered natural talent? Duval couldn't imagine a greater sensation for his audience! So he hires this country bumpkin on the spot for his opera house, where he plans to educate her, and after only a few singing lessons casts her as Norina in Donizetti's *Don Pasquale*. The premiere is a huge success and overnight Thérèse becomes famous. As soon as she has a contract in hand, she confesses to the dumbfounded director that this was not the first time she sang Norina . . .

It is a rare treat to experience Elisabeth Schwarzkopf in this film. A born comedienne, she transforms a sleepy farmer's daughter into an irresistible, eye-catching *prima donna* equipped with razor-thin coloratura and brilliant high notes. There is no doubt that she had the talent for a second career as a film star, for like a true virtuoso she

commanded a light, melodious speaking voice so in vogue in those days—just like Lilian Harvey or Olga Tschechowa. Incidentally, Schwarzkopf once "loaned" her voice to Tschechowa, then the *grande dame* of the German cinema, dubbing her singing scenes in Günther Rittau's drama *Der ewige Klang* (1942–43).

Her last movie role was in Werner Klingler's detective thriller *Der Verteidiger hat das Wort* (1944), where she appeared as an elegant singer who performs Schumann's *Mondnacht* at a soirée. This production was recorded under especially arduous conditions. Icy winds blew through the Ufa-Studio roofs, which had been partially destroyed by bombs, and the hot spotlights had to be constantly switched on and off, causing extreme fluctuations of temperature and profuse perspiration. Consequently, Elisabeth Schwarzkopf developed tuberculosis and had to spend a year convalescing in the Tatra Mountains. Despite her enormous anxiety over her voice, in hindsight this interruption in her career proved to be a stroke of luck since she was spared living in Berlin during the worst year of its wartime bombing.

Three years later, Lillian Fayer became one of the first European photographers to take glamorous photographs of opera singers; until then, such photos had only been made of Hollywood stars. In Elisabeth Schwarzkopf she found an ideal model—a woman who looked similar in type to Marlene Dietrich: it was no accident that some fans dubbed her the "Dietrich of Singing." However, Elisabeth Schwarzkopf never took such comparisons as compliments, for despite her fascination with the visual, she considered only music—quoting Hugo von Hofmannsthal—to be a "holy art." By comparison, film was a profane product of the entertainment industry.

Despite this view, she considered one actress a role model because of her special intonation. It was the Viennese Paula Wessely, whom she saw in 1934 in Willi Forst's film *Maskerade,* and whom she was still enthusing about at the age of eighty-nine: "I admired Wessely for her acting. She spoke with such tone, so naturally and with a certain expression in the sound that you never usually come upon in an actor. As a rule, they convey expression only through spoken words, but she used the sound of the words. It was because of her that I wanted to go to Vienna. Luckily I then got to know her, and that was one of my greatest experiences."

The legendary Mozart Ensemble from the Wiener Staatsoper offered Elisabeth Schwarzkopf an ideal fresh start after the war, in every respect. There she met like-minded, first-rate colleagues such as Irmgard Seefried, Sena Jurinac, Erich Kunz, Paul Schöffler, and Otto Edelmann, who—like her—placed great value upon the in-depth study of scores as well as vocal homogeneity and a precise representation of musical meaning in the staging. Josef Krips, who led most of the productions at the Theater an der Wien, the temporary venue for the Wiener Staatsoper, even demanded that every singer try to memorize the entire libretto. Elisabeth Schwarzkopf would rightly view this as an advantage, as she could change roles within the Opera House according to need—from Susanna to the Countess,

Paula Wessely

from Blondchen to Konstanze. The scenery was so limited that the stage was half empty—not for any aesthetic reasons as is often the case today, but as a result of scarcity and necessity.

The Croatian soprano Sena Jurinac was Cherubino in *Figaro* and Octavian in Strauss's *Rosenkavalier*, and was a regular singer of "trouser roles" in the ensemble. At eighty-five she was one of the last surviving witnesses of the age, and despite the great deprivation and melancholy during the first performances after the war, she nevertheless recalled those times with fondness: "The audience had forgotten that they had to wrap up in hats and blankets due to the icy cold in the theater. We had no props, and also nothing else to put on, and we would search together for some rags, but we were so deeply involved in our characters that nobody missed anything."

Continuing into the 1950s and 1960s, under the direction of such exquisite, skilled musical minds as Oscar Fritz Schuh, Rudolf Hartmann, Günther Rennert, Herbert Graf, and Gustav Rudolf Sellner, in Vienna as well as Salzburg, those staged productions supported the music and not the other way around (which is often the case today). Nor were those productions old-fashioned or musty. It was the liveliness of the characters that stood out, and this was partly due to the artists' lack of vanity: Their representations were placed in the service of the composers and the respective works. This is in stark contrast to so many contemporary directors, who seem so often to consider themselves more important than the pieces, and who interfere with the libretti in attempting to add completely new interpretations. Elisabeth Schwarzkopf made no secret of her rejection of this type of theater direction, the so-called *Regietheater*, which went against her artistic convictions and seemed arrogant and nonsensical.

She also demanded from her students the complete congruence of musical expression with physical gestures. The character of an aria or a song must be reflected in the facial expression. Occasionally, however, she also criticized an excessive insertion of theatricality: "Now you make a terribly sad face, but that is not enough. Above all, I must *hear* that you are sad. If you do not find the right sound, everything else is in vain." She also shared these convictions with the influential British record producer for EMI, Walter Legge, whom she got to know in 1946 in Vienna and married in 1953. Legge, nine years her elder, became equally her manager, mentor, and promoter. He brought her to the most exclusive opera houses—to Covent Garden in London, to La Scala in Milan, and to the Salzburger Festspielhaus, as well as to the biggest concert halls in America. He had a huge impact upon the life of the soprano: He showed her how to make the best use of her voice as a lyric soprano, advised her in her choices of operatic roles, worked meticulously with her on the expression of German lieder, and encouraged her ambitions and her perfectionism.

Elisabeth Schwarzkopf's hardest role was Donna Elvira in *Don Giovanni,* which, after the Marschallin, was the role she performed most frequently—around eighty-five times. Over the course of the decades she gave her a multitude of different faces. Her first Elvira was a lady with a passionate temperament, as revealed at a guest appearance of the Wiener Staatsoper at Covent Garden, London, in 1947–48 and at the legendary production (also released on record) at the Salzburg Festival in 1950, under Wilhelm Furtwängler. Photographs by Lillian Fayer show her as a "Carmen type" with black wig and mantilla (p. 47). In order to appear especially intimidating in a series of performances Elisabeth Schwarzkopf wore a false, elongated nose (p. 66). This was one experiment, however, that she found unconvincing.

It was Herbert von Karajan, in the summer of 1960, who wanted a new image for his Elvira for the Salzburg Festival. He represented her as an elegant, blond, and even querulous lady of the world, to counter the dark, hot-tempered Donna Anna portrayed by Leontyne Price. Elisabeth Schwarzkopf did indeed accept this makeup, but she did not like the new "soft" Elvira with a blond wig. Although Lillian Fayer's portraits are predominantly strong in facial expression, they nevertheless also show her as a woman who looked more delicate and vulnerable, but still always very passionate (p. 81).

Indeed, whether blond or brunette, in the long run Elvira was a figure who remained foreign to Elisabeth Schwarzkopf all her life: "I am not even sure myself whether I like her," she said, "but Elvira directed my path in life. She made me exceed myself by demanding extremes."

It was Elisabeth Schwarzkopf's harsh self-criticism again that caused her repertoire to diminish over the years. After she heard Maria Callas she no longer wanted to sing Traviata, Gilda, Mimi, or Madame Butterfly. The only character in the Italian repertory that she held onto was Alice Ford in Verdi's *Falstaff*, an almost Mozartian light-comedy figure.

How wonderful that Walter Legge was nonetheless successful in convincing his wife to make a joint recording with Callas: In Puccini's *Turandot* Schwarzkopf sang the part of Liù—deeply heart-rending and with heavenly head tones in the upper register. She also sang Elisabeth in *Tannhäuser*, Elsa in *Lohengrin*, and Leonore in a concert performance of *Fidelio*, but she performed these roles only a few times. She felt that her lyrical voice was not penetrating and powerful enough to adapt to these more dramatic characters. Later, she particularly did not want to discuss these roles and—something difficult indeed for even the trained ear to comprehend—the way she shaped the arias and monologues of the characters with such immense expression and devotion, attested to by those precious and rare recordings.

At the end only Donna Elvira, Fiordiligi, and the Countesses in *Figaro* and *Capriccio* remained, as well as the role with which the singer made history and also presented on screen at the zenith of her career: the Marschallin.

In fact, Elisabeth Schwarzkopf was recorded twice on film in this role. Paul Czinner[2] immortalized Schwarzkopf's Marschallin—unfortunately only in the pre-recorded (with lip-synching) method customary at the time—in the legendary 1960 Salzburg *Rosenkavalier* under Karajan, with which the Grosses Festspielhaus was inaugurated. Then in 1961 the BBC made a studio

recording[3] of Elisabeth Schwarzkopf and Hertha Töpper performing the finale of the first act with the Philharmonia Orchestra under Charles Mackerras. This black-and-white film directed by Patricia Foy is the better of the two because it was recorded "live" (without dubbing) and, moreover, because Elisabeth Schwarzkopf was even more touching—as she herself believed—in her expression of melancholy and wistful contemplation.

Vienna, Salzburg, London, Milan, Paris, San Francisco, New York, Buenos Aires: Elisabeth Schwarzkopf performed the Marschallin in almost every metropolis and also starred throughout the world as an "ambassador of German lieder." She also returned to her artistic roots in Berlin with a farewell lieder recital in 1978. Thus she closed the circle at the Deutsche Oper Berlin where she had begun with her debut performance as the Flower Maiden forty years earlier. It was a grand evening, with many encores and standing ovations. It was also the one and only time I experienced the great singer on stage: I was enthralled by her voice and her aura.

Lillian Fayer cited as one of Elisabeth Schwarzkopf's greatest assets the fact that she never put on airs. I completely concur. From the very start I was surprised by her unconventional manner. She often called me spontaneously, as she did following the first time I wrote to request an interview in 1994. At that time, I was still a trainee at the Bavarian Radio and inexperienced in talking to celebrities. One day a secretary there handed me the telephone receiver and said, "Frau Liese,

---

[2] Available on DVD from RCA Red Seal (BMG).

[3] Available on DVD from EMI Classics in "Legend: Elisabeth Schwarzkopf—Strauss."

a Frau Schwarzkopf would like to speak to you." When I tried to express my delight and overcome my nerves about speaking to her in person, the Diva said only, "Come on, it's not so bad."

Mostly I was impressed by the magnanimity she displayed in the interview when we came to speak about why she never played Strauss's Arabella on stage. Now it is common to associate this role with Schwarzkopf's "archrival"—the Swiss prima donna Lisa Della Casa, who made operatic history as "Arabellissima." In this respect it was a somewhat delicate question. Elisabeth Schwarzkopf's fairness and collegiality were expressed in her answer: "The opportunity never arose, but it is no misfortune. There are others who have performed the role splendidly, better than I would have been able to."

Elisabeth Schwarzkopf was altogether a valuable witness of her times. She was acquainted with almost all the famous musicians and singers of the epoch, except one: Sergiu Celibidache. It seems as though he could have been predestined as her soulmate: a constant perfectionist and tinkerer in all questions of sound and, like her, one who considered Furtwängler his greatest colleague at the conductor's podium. On the other hand, the Romanian only jeered contemptuously at Karajan: "He has mass popularity—so does Coca-Cola."

Indeed, Elisabeth Schwarzkopf sang for a decade under Karajan, but she later came to regret it—because at the request of "Mr. K" she took on many roles that she regarded as unsuited to her type of voice and found him personally disappointing. In 1964 Karajan got rid of her without any justification. Discreet as Elisabeth Schwarzkopf was, she did not shout it from the rooftops: "Some people have naturally flawed characters," she sighed, and agreed with me that it is a shame she never met Celibidache in her concert career. Perhaps that was the only omission. In the long run, luck was always on Elisabeth Schwarzkopf's side. At one of her last public appearances in November 2004, for an interview at the completely sold-out Wiener Staatsoper, it was the same as ever. The audience did not want to let Dame Elisabeth (as the English Queen had officially dubbed her) depart. Emotional and almost disbelieving, she thanked them for the many flowers and the standing ovation. Upon parting she had one eye laughing, the other tearful. She left the stage empty, as though making way for the next generation. *"Ist halt vorbei."* ("Well, it's over.") Elisabeth Schwarzkopf *was* the Marschallin.

Kirsten Liese

About three years old in Jarotschin, with her grandmother Marie Fröhlich.

Around 1923.

"Poppi" with his guitar, inspiring his daughter's passion for singing and her love for the Czech national composer, Bedřich Smetana.

From country bumpkin to opera diva: stills from the twenty-one-minute film *Das Mädchen von Saint Coeur*, by Bernhard Wentzel, Berlin, 1940.

Becoming famous overnight as Norina in Donizetti's *Don Pasquale*: Elisabeth Schwarzkopf as Thérèse de Lorm in the film *Das Mädchen von Saint Coeur*.

As Zerbinetta in Strauss's *Ariadne auf Naxos* at the Deutsches Opernhaus Berlin. Through this 1940 production she met someone who became an important influence on her future, the baritone Karl Schmitt-Walter, who told her, "Miss Schwarzkopf, you are such a great talent, but you have absolutely no technique, and that simply cannot be." He put her in touch with the famous singing coach Maria Ivogün, who initiated significant developments in Schwarzkopf's later international career.

In 1941, as understudy for a colleague taken ill, Elisabeth Schwarzkopf sings the title role in *Undine*, Albert Lortzing's romantic and magical opera. She learned the role in an underground bomb shelter during the war.

In Werner Klingler's crime comedy *Der Verteidiger hat das Wort*, 1944.

Elisabeth Schwarzkopf as Konstanze in Mozart's opera *Die Entführung aus dem Serail*, which ran from 1946 to 1948 at the Theater an der Wien, the temporary home of the bombed-out Wiener Staatsoper. The Pasha Selim at her side is the renowned stage actor Paul Hubschmid.

She played Susanna in Mozart's *Le nozze di Figaro* only a few times—in 1947 and then early in 1948 at the Theater an der Wien. Then in August 1948, for the first time singing under Karajan, she switched to the Countess Almaviva. At her side is Erich Kunz as Figaro.

With the conductor Josef Krips, who directed the legendary Vienna Mozart Ensemble after the Second World War. Elisabeth Schwarzkopf counted him among the leading conductors of her time, and the one she esteemed the most after Furtwängler.

"I am a realistic person," said Elisabeth Schwarzkopf of herself at age eighty-nine. The photographs Lillian Fayer took in 1947 (here and on the three preceding pages) show a very tender, sensitive woman who over the years fashioned internal armor to protect herself from the hardships of her profession.

Richard Strauss's *Der Rosenkavalier* accompanied Elisabeth Schwarzkopf throughout her entire singing career. Before she took up the role with which she is identified to this day—the Marschallin—she had already played other parts in that opera. In 1938, at the Deutsches Opernhaus in Berlin, she sang the first of the Three Noble Orphans, followed—a decade later—by the role of Sophie, which she performed for the first time in 1948 in Vienna at the Theater an der Wien. This photo presumably dates from that time.

As Marzelline in Beethoven's *Fidelio* at Covent Garden, London, 1950.

For the reopening of the Bayreuth Festival in 1951, Elisabeth Schwarzkopf took on the role of Eva in *Die Meistersinger von Nürnberg*. It is her only major Wagner role that she—always the most self-critical perfectionist—remembered with pleasure.

Igor Stravinsky thanks his "Anne Trulove" with a
kiss on the hand after the premiere of his opera
The Rake's Progress at the Teatro La Fenice in
Venice (1951). In the background is Stravinsky's
old friend, the Russian-American composer
Nicolas Nabokov. Elisabeth Schwarzkopf
recalled this production with mixed feelings: At
the premiere, Stravinsky remained completely
glued to the score and failed to give the singers
any of their cues. Luckily, the eminently skilled
Ferdinand Leitner had conducted the rehearsals
so the production was a triumph.

Star portrait from the 1950s.

This snapshot was probably taken in 1951 in Bayreuth, where Elisabeth Schwarzkopf learned the role of Anne Trulove for the Stravinsky premiere, between performances of *Die Meistersinger von Nürnberg, Das Rheingold,* and *Götterdämmerung.*

Elisabeth Schwarzkopf loved the mountains and was an ardent skier. These two photographs were probably taken in the late 1940s in the Austrian village of Schruns, where she also spent the last three years of her life.

Newly wed to Walter Legge, in their garden in London, 1953.

This photograph was also taken in London in the early 1950s, showing Elisabeth Schwarzkopf with their Siamese cats, which were born under the lid of her piano!

Trying on a hat—a snapshot taken in San Francisco, September 1955.

On October 25, 1953, Elisabeth Schwarzkopf makes her U.S. debut with a highly acclaimed lieder recital at New York's Town Hall. She is accompanied by the Hungarian pianist Arpád Sándor.

Elisabeth Schwarzkopf, piano legend Gerald Moore (left), and Walter Legge presented an inseparable trio. They recorded songs in London for fifteen years. "Walter has a good ear," said Moore, "and mine is also not bad. But only Elisabeth hears things that nobody else can. She would hear the grass growing!" In this photograph they concentrate together on listening to a studio recording.

As Donna Elvira in Mozart's *Don Giovanni*, 1954.

With Cesare Siepi as the irresistible seducer in the legendary *Don Giovanni* at the Salzburger Felsenreitschule under Wilhelm Furtwängler (1954).

Giovanni: *Come, come, dear Donna Elvira, don't be angry with me! Listen, let me explain.*

Elvira: *How can you excuse such vileness? You worm your way into my house . . . and leave me prey to remorse and grief, to punish me, no doubt, for loving you so much!*

Sequence from the "Catalogue Aria": As
Leporello, at Elisabeth Schwarzkopf's side, is the
brilliant Austrian baritone Otto Edelmann.
Leporello: *Young lady, this is the list of the ladies
my master has loved; . . . read it with me.*

Leporello: . . . one hundred in France, in Turkey ninety-one, but in Spain already one thousand and three!

Leporello: *You know what he'll do!*

As the Countess Almaviva in Mozart's *Le nozze di Figaro*, Salzburg, 1957.

As the Countess Almaviva in Mozart's *Le nozze di Figaro*, Teatro alla Scala, 1954.

An on-the-set "taster course": In this photograph of Elisabeth Schwarzkopf as the Countess, taken in 1957 at the Salzburger Festspielhaus, the twelve-year-old Andreas Barylli plays the part of a second lighting assistant to his mother, Lillian Fayer.

As the Countess Almaviva in Mozart's *Le nozze di Figaro*, Salzburg, 1957.

A *Figaro* dream couple: Elisabeth Schwarzkopf
and Dietrich Fischer-Dieskau as Countess and
Count at the Salzburg Festival in 1957.

A sequence from the second act of *Figaro* with Dietrich Fischer-Dieskau: the Count and the Countess in a marital row.
The Count: *What is that noise? Something fell in your room.*
The Countess: *I heard nothing.*
The Count: *You must have weighty matters on your mind.*
The Countess: *Of what?*
The Count: *There's someone there.*

The Count: *I can go myself and bring the tools without any outcry . . . You will have the goodness to come with me. Let me offer you my arm, Madam, let's go.*

The Count: *Give me the key!*
The Countess: *He is innocent and you know it . . .*
The Count: *I know nothing of the sort. Hence from my sight! You are faithless; you've sought to disgrace me.*

A scene from the third act of *Figaro* with Fischer-
Dieskau:
The Count: *Such presumption!*
The Countess: *I am petrified . . . Here are the
two betrothed couples, we must receive them. One
especially has your protection.*

An ideal stage partner for Elisabeth Schwarzkopf in this Salzburg *Figaro*, Irmgard Seefried sings the role of Susanna (left). Here they perform the duet "How sweet the breeze will be this evening in the pine grove."

Elisabeth Schwarzkopf with pianist Gerald Moore
at the end of the 1950s.

This snapshot with Gerald Moore
was taken at a Salzburg tavern
toward the end of the 1950s.

As Alice Ford in Verdi's *Falstaff*, Salzburg, 1957.

As Elsa in Wagner's *Lohengrin*, Vienna, 1958.

An unusual experiment: Schwarzkopf as Elvira with an artificial nose, Vienna, 1958.

Walter Legge, EMI record producer, signed all
the great musicians and singers of the twentieth
century, including the cellist Pablo Casals, who
died in 1973. Casals is shown here with Elisabeth
Schwarzkopf in the late 1950s.

Two ideally harmonized on-stage sisters: As Fiordiligi and Dorabella in Mozart's *Così fan tutte*, Elisabeth Schwarzkopf and Christa Ludwig set a new standard in Salzburg (left, 1958; right, 1960).

The third among an exquisite trio of ladies in
the Salzburg *Così*: the Italian soubrette Graziella
Sciutti (center) as Despina, the carefree
chambermaid (1958).

A scene from Mozart's *Così*, directed by Günther Rennert (1960), with the two sisters and Despina, disguised as a doctor (Graziella Sciutti, center), and Ferrando (Waldemar Kmentt), still somewhat dazed after a feigned suicide attempt.

Two scenes from the second act of
Mozart's *Così*, Salzburg, 1960.

Dorabella: *I'll take the little dark
one, who seems wittier to me.*
Fiordiligi: *And, meanwhile, with the blond
one, I want to laugh and joke a little.*

Fiordiligi: *In a few moments I will be in the arms of my faithful betrothed; unrecognizable in these clothes, I will come before him.*

This photograph of Maria Callas and Elisabeth
Schwarzkopf probably dates from 1957, the
year they recorded Puccini's *Turandot* together.

Again with Maria Callas, the *primadonna assoluta*.

An unusual foray into baroque opera: As early as 1959—long before the historic-revival movement—the Teatro alla Scala presented Handel's rarely staged scenic oratorio *Hercules*, with Elisabeth Schwarzkopf as Iole. Her partner in this photograph is the mezzo-soprano Fedora Barbieri in the role of Deianeira.

A portrait, 1958.

With her parents, probably in the mid-1950s.

With her father, probably in the mid-1950s.

A new look: At Herbert von Karajan's request, Elisabeth Schwarzkopf appears with a blond wig as Elvira in Mozart's *Don Giovanni*. Above, with Leontyne Price as Donna Anna, Salzburg, 1960.

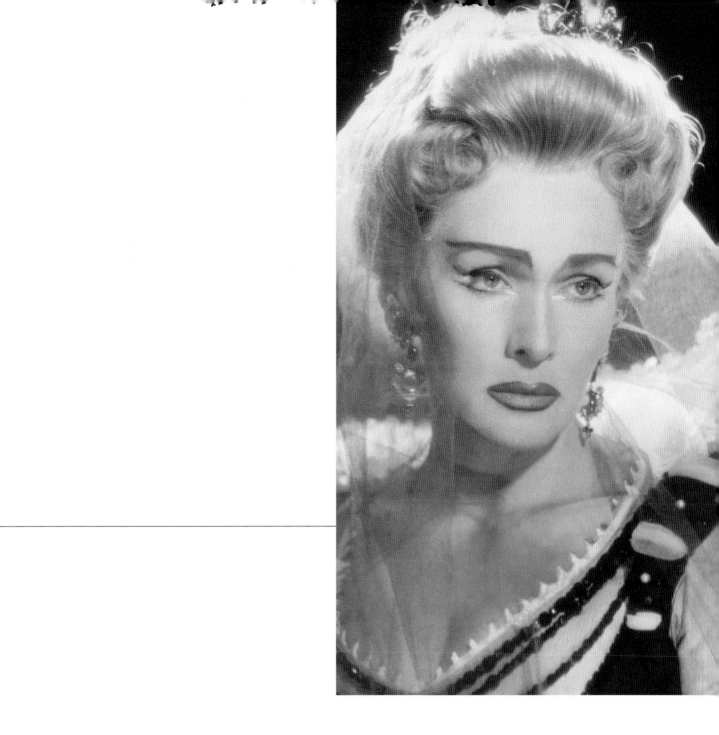

Star portraits as the Marschallin in
Strauss's *Rosenkavalier* in London,
Salzburg, and Vienna, 1959 and 1961.

A dream cast: Elisabeth Schwarzkopf
as the Marschallin and Anneliese
Rothenberger as Sophie, Vienna, 1961.
Marschallin: *Don't talk too much,
you are pretty enough as it is.*

A scene from the first act of *Der Rosenkavalier*, with Sena Jurinac as Octavian/"Mariandl" and Otto Edelmann as Baron Ochs.

The Salzburg *Rosenkavalier*, which opened the
Grosses Festspielhaus in 1960 under Herbert
von Karajan, is legendary. More performances
followed in 1961. This photograph shows
Christa Ludwig, Elisabeth Schwarzkopf, and Otto
Edelmann during applause after the first act.

Undeniably gifted as an actress, Elisabeth
Schwarzkopf smiles coyly in this scene from *Der
Rosenkavalier.*

This glorious silver-colored silk dress with a purple velvet cloak made costume history when it was worn by Elisabeth Schwarzkopf in the Salzburg *Rosenkavalier*. It was the diva's personal possession.

In front of a BBC camera as the Marschallin in a London studio production of the first act of *Der Rosenkavalier* (1961).

The Countess Madeleine in *Capriccio* was
the last significant Strauss role that Elisabeth
Schwarzkopf included in her repertoire, and
one of the best. After her appearance in
1959 in London, *The Times* wrote: "Here the
singer, the role and the vocalisation were at
one—human, intent on truth and beauty, and
truly interpretative." Lillian Fayer took her
photograph in this role in Vienna in 1960.

The "Dispute Ensemble" scene in *Capriccio*: From left to right: Hermann Uhde (the Count), Christel Goltz (Clairon), Elisabeth Schwarzkopf (the Countess), Paul Schöffler (La Roche, the theater director), Walter Berry (Olivier, the poet), and Anton Dermota (Flamand, the musician).

Countess: *Oh, dear! Now they are attacking him [La Roche]! My attempted rescue is an utter failure.*

Clairon: *Don't worry! A fight between men always ends with one victor!*

La Roche: *Give me a chance to speak! You are mistaken! But do listen!*

With the conductor Wolfgang Sawallisch
(left) and fellow singers Eberhard Wächter
(center) and Nicolai Gedda (right)
during the complete studio recording of
Strauss's *Capriccio* in London, 1959.

It is an honor and a great pleasure for me, a musical contemporary witness so to speak, to commemorate Elisabeth Schwarzkopf, together with whom I worked on recordings and as her accompanist in concert hall recitals. I will never forget the hours we spent making music together immediately after the last world war at a recital which took place in the Royal Festival Hall in London, with a program of very special meaning, solely dedicated to the compositions of Hugo Wolf. The beauty of her voice, her personality, her ability to modulate speech and music, and her pure, precise intonation were all subordinated in service to the works themselves and yet she shaped each into a work of distinction, in a singular way that no other artist has achieved or that has ever been surpassed. It is a special kind of gift to have met the greatest singer of the last century.

Wolfgang Sawallisch, Chiemgau, June 10, 2007.

Four star portraits from 1961 and 1962.

King Baudouin of Belgium and his wife, Queen Fabiola, offer their congratulations after a performance of *Der Rosenkavalier* at the Théâtre de la Monnaie in Brussels in 1962.

In one of her last interviews, asked to name her greatest achievement as a singer, the eighty-nine-year-old Elisabeth Schwarzkopf said, "Everything Viennese," by which she also had in mind her numerous operetta roles. In Lillian Fayer's 1962 photograph she poses as Lehár's *Lustige Witwe.*

In her time, Elisabeth Schwarzkopf was the princess of the opera stage. Her silver voice so wonderfully matched such theatrical characters as the Countess in *Capriccio* and Mozart's *Le nozze di Figaro* or the Marschallin in *Der Rosenkavalier*. Her singing was high art, always informed by the mind. Her sophisticated interpretations of texts enabled her to use her voice to represent the content and meaning of the songs. Her entire life was shaped by her occupation. Many of her pupils went away in tears, but many could profit from her art because she always set the highest standards for herself and others. Her art has been of huge benefit to me.

Christa Ludwig, Vienna, June 16, 2007.

With Christa Ludwig in Salzburg, 1962.

At the request of Herbert von Karajan, Elisabeth Schwarzkopf takes on the role of Elisabeth in Wagner's *Tannhäuser* in Vienna in 1962.

A lieder recital with Dietrich Fischer-Dieskau
(right) and Gerald Moore at Carnegie Hall,
New York, 1964. Hugo Wolf's *Italienisches
Liederbuch* was included in the program. "He
was our guiding star," said Elisabeth Schwarzkopf
of Fischer-Dieskau, whom she admired
the most among her singing colleagues.

A snapshot taken in Santander, Spain, where Elisabeth Schwarzkopf made a guest appearance at a lieder recital in 1965.

Wearing a dirndl, amid ancient holy shrines. This exotic photograph was probably taken in Baalbek, Lebanon, where Elisabeth Schwarzkopf gave a lieder recital in July 1966.

A star portrait from 1965, which Elisabeth Schwarzkopf often sent as an autographed card.

In the mid-sixties Schwarzkopf and her husband, Walter Legge, moved from London to Ascona on Lake Maggiore. However, this location proved unfavorable: the nearest convenient airport was constantly closed, and concert travel became difficult. Soon after, Legge purchased a villa at Lake Geneva, which he and his wife christened "Le Petit Port" ("The Little Harbor"). This photograph shows the couple there, at the beginning of the 1970s.

"It seems to me quite unfair for anyone to look so ravishing and sing so beautifully," Gerald Moore once said of Elisabeth Schwarzkopf. The pianist, who shared his secrets for posterity as a lieder accompanist in his book *Am I Too Loud?*, took leave of his audience at a farewell concert in 1967 at London's Royal Festival Hall. That legendary concert, "A Tribute to Gerald Moore," arranged by Walter Legge, was also immortalized in a live recording (available now on CD). Three favorite singing partners—Elisabeth Schwarzkopf, the Catalan soprano Victoria de los Angeles, and baritone Dietrich Fischer-Dieskau, whom Moore called a "genius"—appeared at this homage to "accompany" the pianist not only as soloists but also in duets and trios.

From left to right: Gerald Moore, Elisabeth
Schwarzkopf, Victoria de los Angeles,
and Dietrich Fischer-Dieskau.

Dear Elisabeth, wherever you are, no doubt you are smiling as you watch the preparations for this book—all these people bustling about to get the smallest details right and be worthy of your sense of perfection. But I can also imagine a slight frown and your comment, "You'd better listen to my recordings rather than spend all that time on a book with photographs; after all I was known for my voice and not for my good looks." Of course your voice was unique, but so was your beauty. "And she can sing, too?" were the words of doubt pronounced by an amazed member of the audience at one of your first American recitals as soon as you arrived on stage. These numerous photographs not only bring to life again your Marschallin, your Fiordiligi, your Countess in *Figaro*—to mention only the few parts in which I saw and heard you in the flesh—but also revive fond memories of lunches in the garden, car rides around Europe, and moments of relaxation. I must laugh when I look at my albums and the many pictures I took of you photographing daffodils, tulips, peonies, or gladioli, facing the photos you took of me in the same activity. The competition was tough, but your shots were better than mine. Your eye always captured the ideal moment and the ideal angle. Photography was one of your many talents, and with good reason you called yourself an *Augenmensch* (visual person). For forty years of friendship—in the final words of Richard Strauss's *"Zueignung"* ("Dedication")—*Habe Dank!* Thank you.

Claire Erlanger, Geneva, July 10, 2007.

On holiday in Gargellen near the Austrian village of Schruns, June 1967: This photograph from the private album of Claire Erlanger, Walter Legge's longtime secretary and a good family friend, provides a glimpse of Elisabeth Schwarzkopf as amateur photographer and animal lover.

In March 1968, along with the then little-known pianist Alfred Brendel (left), Elisabeth Schwarzkopf records Mozart's concert aria "*Ch'io mi scordi di te*" for soprano, solo piano, and orchestra. In the background: Walter Legge and George Szell (right), director of these recording sessions with the London Symphony Orchestra.

In April 1968 Elisabeth Schwarzkopf launched her first Japanese tour with her accompanist Geoffrey Parsons. In this photograph the two sign autographs at the end of a lieder recital in Tokyo.

Smile and say "cheese": Wherever the famous duo showed their faces during their tour of Japan, everyone wanted a picture taken with them.

Snack time at the Grand Saint Bernard Pass en route from "Le Petit Port" to Milan, April 1970.

The honorary doctorate: On June 10, 1976, she became Elisabeth Schwarzkopf, hon. D. Mus., at Cambridge University.

Schwarzkopf the gourmet, at "Le Petit
Port" with a lemon mousse, May 1970.

Lieder recital in December 1976.

A lieder recital with the pianist Geoffrey
Parsons, most likely in the 1970s.

A master class at the Britten-Pears School in Aldeburgh, England, during the early 1980s.

In a photograph taken during the 1980s, Elisabeth Schwarzkopf is greeted by the French conductor Georges Prêtre in Paris. These two collaborated on performances of *Capriccio* in Vienna, Paris, and San Francisco between 1962 and 1964.

Elisabeth Schwarzkopf received many awards, including the Ordre pour le Mérite in 1984. In this photograph she is shown during the ceremony at the University of Bonn with Kurt Bittel, vice-chancellor of the order.

Elisabeth Schwarzkopf gave lieder recitals in France in 1969, 1971, and 1973, accompanied by the Italian pianist Aldo Ciccolini. At the Villa Schindler in October 2004, the two artists were joyfully reunited after thirty years.

The great regard, respect, and friendship that Elisabeth Schwarzkopf showed for the conductor Wilhelm Furtwängler were fully reciprocated. His widow, Elisabeth Furtwängler, also held her in high esteem. The two ladies fondly telephoned each other often. "Wilhelm said there is no better singer than Schwarzkopf," recalled Mme. Furtwängler, in a book by the music journalist Klaus Lang. The date and setting of this photo of the two namesakes are unknown.

The recollection of the performances—whether at the opera or in concert—in which Wilhelm Furtwängler collaborated with Elisabeth Schwarzkopf still fills me today with great gratitude. Furtwängler was very fortunate in these performances. Her great musicality facilitated their joint work. Whether performing Mozart or Beethoven, Elisabeth Schwarzkopf's colleagues were also happy to have in her such a reliable partner. In 1953 there was a *Liederabend* devoted to Hugo Wolf on the program at the Salzburg Festival, and the scheduled accompanist—for reasons I can no longer recall—was canceled. With some diffidence Wilhelm Furtwängler asked whether Madame Schwarzkopf would accept him as her accompanist. She accepted with enthusiasm. I remember that my husband had to prepare intensively for this concert and that he had some stage fright beforehand, which to him was something otherwise totally alien. Well, the evening was a great success. Also contributing to Elisabeth Schwarzkopf's successes was her beauty. The vision of her onstage, in conjunction with her vocal artistry, inspired the public. I personally treasured as well her humanity, which she radiated. Dear Elisabeth, you remain unforgotten. Thank you.

Elisabeth Furtwängler

Ever since our first meeting in 1969, I have been living under a spell cast by the personality of Elisabeth Schwarzkopf. Tirelessly pursuing the course chosen together with her husband and mentor, Walter Legge, she knew how to combine her exceptional vocal mastery, her elegance, and her clear comprehension of the poet's words with a feeling and sensitivity way beyond the norm. But despite all her extraordinary abilities, I was struck by her humility when confronting a musical score, her capacity to grasp the slightest musical inflection within, her profound comprehension through which she found the means to express the inexpressible, and to serve the music with her sheer will to work that was intoxicating to behold. Through the memories of our musical encounters, but also thanks to the ample evidence—both visual and resonant—that Elisabeth has given us, I find confirmation of the two principal qualities shared by the greatest of all artists: talent and exacting standards.

Aldo Ciccolini, Asnières, July 2, 2007.

A Romantic impression in the style of the painter
Caspar David Friedrich: Elisabeth Schwarzkopf
was a keen photographer, especially of flowers.
She counted this example, with Walter Legge
in the background, as her most successful.

MARGARET 1891
WALTER LEGGE
1906-1979
ELISABETH
SCHWARZKOPF-LEGGE
1915-2006

Elisabeth Schwarzkopf died on August
3, 2006. She was buried in the family
grave in Zumikon, outside Zürich, beside
her husband and her parents.

Elisabeth Schwarzkopf? I met her only a few times, and at these enjoyable meetings I was struck by a deep sense of awe. She was generous and helpful toward the young singers who met her high standards, and her praise—her appreciation—was an unforgettable incentive. The great art of Elisabeth Schwarzkopf is permanently inscribed, or "intoned," in the annals of the immortal goddesses of singing. My memory of her is imprinted with great esteem, admiration, and respect for her extreme discipline and self-criticism. I am convinced that she now passes on her paramount skill and knowledge to carefully chosen angels, who will endlessly profit from it (if they do not precipitously quit the clouds with tears in their eyes).

Brigitte Fassbaender, Innsbruck, June 25, 2007.

The first time I met Elisabeth Schwarzkopf was in 1961, when I was making my debut as Nannetta in Verdi's *Falstaff* at Covent Garden.

I considered her one of the greatest artists to serve as an inspiration for my career, and when she visited me in my dressing room after the performance I was overcome with emotion at our first most felicitous meeting. Only years later did I learn that shortly after that encounter in London Elisabeth had suggested to the then superintendent at La Scala to engage me for my debut at the famous Milan theater!

This was a gesture not only of a great and generous artist but, above all, of a true friend, and that is how I recall Elisabeth.

Mirella Freni

Elisabeth Schwarzkopf, Rita Streich, and I were all pupils of Maria Ivogün, who exclusively developed the three of us into high sopranos. I idolized Elisabeth Schwarzkopf, and she was my role model in so many parts. When I sang my first Susanna [in Mozart's *Nozze di Figaro*] at the Wiener Staatsoper, she was my Countess—unfortunately her last performance in that role, while my first as her maid. Yet Elisabeth Schwarzkopf gave me a charming gift for good luck on stage ("Break a leg!"): a hairbrush which she always carried and which today I still keep in my vanity case!

Renate Holm, Vienna, 2008.

Elisabeth Schwarzkopf was a standard. The standards that Elisabeth Schwarzkopf maintained for herself through an almost unimaginable regime of self-discipline, and that she so passionately and uncompromisingly insisted upon from her students and even fellow colleagues, are the essence of my memory of her. Her unfailing ability to assess, question, rethink, and rethink again essential questions of poetry, music, tone, and their effectual relevance to one another was remarkable. Hours of work together seemed like fleeting moments but even now resonate in my artistic judgments like a mantra learned long ago. For her sharing with me her passion, her sense of beauty, and her singular sense of artistic purpose in the most gracious, generous, and, yes, at times austere ways, I will be eternally grateful.

Thomas Hampson, Vienna, July 4, 2007.

Epilogue

A Pilgrimage to Schruns: Elisabeth Schwarzkopf at Ninety

Charles Scribner III

Monday, January 30, 2006

This morning I landed in Paris en route to Zürich, the first airborne leg of my pilgrimage to Schruns, in Vorarlberg, Austria, to visit Dame Elisabeth Schwarzkopf. She has lived in Schruns these past three years, under a glistening tiara of snow-capped Alps, ever since moving from her house in Zumikon, outside Zürich. I had hoped to time my visit to celebrate her ninetieth birthday last month, but a family obligation drew me westward to the Rockies when I wanted to soar like Strauss orchestrations through the Alps.

So now I finally arrive on the heels of Mozart's 250th birthday, his *bicenquinquagenary*, a term I discovered at a Princeton University celebration a decade ago. Mozart was born in the year that Nassau Hall—the center of the Princeton campus—was completed.

But I digress. I blame not only jet lag but the immediate surroundings. I am sitting in an old inn called the Hemingway beside the village church of St. Jodok, so refreshing in its sorbet hues and beckoning with its confectionery onion dome atop the bell tower. It's a blessedly short stroll through snowy streets to my hotel, the Zimba, a few houses down from Schwarzkopf's flat on the Veltlinerweg. It's all within a stone's throw of the train station, where I was thrilled to arrive at the end of the Montafonerbahn.

Back home, I had boasted that getting here would take two planes and four trains. I had mis-calculated: the total of trains numbered six—a daunting itinerary to decipher. But I made it—one train at a time, and lots of frantic interviews in between. When in early stages of apprehension I reached Elisabeth via cell phone I confessed that I felt like Tannhäuser setting off on his Roman pilgrimage.

She directed me to raise my sights and look up at the mountains—pitch-perfect advice. Our Rockies cannot compete; these Alps take the gold. As the train passed alongside a lake outside Zürich, the fine mist rising from frigid water cast the magnificent mountain backdrop in a gray-slate haze, a Romantic veil that mirrored a Caspar David Friedrich landscape. Oscar Wilde was right: Art doesn't imitate nature; nature imitates art.

I have never written more than a postcard in a restaurant. But Hemingway's has a long wooden table with no one else sitting there; I might as well be at my desk back home while two neighboring tables of cheerful Austrian skiers provide a steady current of melodic conversation strong enough to ward off my self-consciousness. The waitress stopped and commented that I "write very fast." So perhaps enough self-consciousness has remained to recast me as a student dying to finish his homework before being called out for sacrilege in a tavern.

But then I recalled that my family's most Ernest author used to write in cafés and in fact came to Schruns with his wife Hadley and infant son, and stayed a full six months, long enough to complete his first great novel, *The Sun Also Rises*, an idyllic interlude he later chronicled at the end of *A Moveable Feast*.

I confess I have always admired Hemingway's style more than his substance, or at least his subject matter, the latter so often featuring unbecoming self-postures. But he certainly proved the capacity and value of writing "one true sentence." He did it over and over. His legacy, for now, seems secure; he was more celebrated at his recent centennial in 1999 than Mozart was at his in 1856, 150 years ago. Of course, I'll have no way of knowing whether Hemingway will survive as long or as gloriously. *"Il faut d'abord durer"* was his driving motto—"First, one must endure." So far so good.

I was reminded of that literary footnote as I boarded my fourth train—from Buchs to Feldkirch—which would transport us from Switzerland, through Liechtenstein, and finally across the border into Austria. Its side was emblazoned *The Ernest Hemingway*; I knew at last I was on the right track. Hemingway's centennial had illustrated the fruits of his favorite maxim: He has endured.

But today that footnote belongs to the impeccable Dame Elisabeth: At ninety she has been justly hailed the greatest singer of Mozart in the second half of the past century, certainly for my lifetime and arguably her own as well. That is my thesis to be inked and underscored on the pristine cream-colored pages of this leather-bound, gold-stamped journal that my bride, Ritchie, gave me as a wedding gift more that twenty-six years ago, in the summer of 1979.

The pages, edged in gold, have remained blank all these years, for want of a worthy subject. But all in God's good time: As I packed for my trip, I didn't want to sit beside Elisabeth and take notes on some paltry pad of paper. Then I spotted this slim blue leather volume nestled on a shelf next to my favorite opera books. *Ecco!*

Its gold-stamped year, 1979, was as sad for Elisabeth as it was happy for me. That was the year her husband, Walter Legge, died just three days after her farewell concert, at the close of which he had proclaimed her "a bloody miracle." Through my five decades of listening she has projected into sound the absolute ideal of beauty—what Shakespeare called "the constant image."

Tonight, a few minutes before my arrival, Elisabeth called the Hotel Zimba and ordered a bottle of wine for me. The young woman at the desk spoke hardly a word of English as she tried to explain that "Professor Dr. Schwarzkopf" had sent a bottle of wine to my room as a welcome gift. The only words that came to my mind were Octavian's (disguised as the maid Mariandl) in the last act of *Der Rosenkavalier*: *"Nein, nein, nein, nein! I trink' kein Wein."*

But here my wine had been ordered not by the lecherous Baron Ochs but the Marschallin herself, to whom in another life I would have dearly loved to play her Octavian. I confessed that I didn't drink wine and would be so grateful to have a bottle of mineral water instead. Turning wine into water took no miracle tonight—but it did take some diplomatic explaining. Dame Elisabeth is today a much sought-out and celebrated professor of voice, but tonight her fine-tuned grace suddenly conjured up earlier scenes from Mozart and Strauss; to me, she embodies both the Countess and the Marschallin.

I am to stop by her house tomorrow morning at 11:30, for our first face-to-face visit in two decades. I shall try to do her justice, as I promised, on the subject of Mozart. She and Mozart inhabit special niches in my pantheon of music: all air and light. "*Dove sono i bei momenti?*"

Here, tomorrow, God willing. I pray I may preserve a sampling of that precious past in print. Ours is surely the last generation to do so in longhand. How I'd love to give a blank book as elegant as this one to my sons, but they would never use it. Their blank pages are in cyberspace.

Tuesday, January 31, 2006

Sitting almost alone in the breakfast room of the Zimba—most of the other guests have already taken to the slopes—I can see through the lightly draped picture windows the Alps and patches of the clearest blue skies I can recall. I am sure I have seen as blue in Maine or even Florida, but here the backdrop of the Alps and the reflections of the snow-capped peaks work their morning magic—and long beyond first light.

I have almost two hours until I walk over to Elisabeth's. Time to meander in daylight and daydream about an excursion up the mountains. I worried last night about how I would pass the time when Elisabeth was not free to discuss Mozart. In the clear light of day such worries are soon dispelled.

I picked up in the hotel lobby a colorful brochure from Pfefferkorn's, traditional local woodcarvers with an array of objects for sale—from clowns to crucifixes. The cover has captivated me: a wind-tossed, bearded, and unusually youthful St. Christopher carrying the Christ Child, who tugs at the saint's beard as the tyke holds on for dear life. I'll go out and see whether there is a version for sale here in Schruns. The village church does not have daily mass, and I need something tangible for my prayers each day for my own beloved son Christopher, an ocean away.

The church of St. Jodok is magnificent, a polychrome Baroque feast of wood carving—the Pfefferkorn brochure writ large. There was no mass this morning, but somehow the space, so freezing that the font of holy water was covered by a sheet of ice, seemed even more suited to a votive candle at the Virgin's altar. I was able to make out enough of the German prayer to leave my flickering candle as a silent sacrament to light the rest of the day. And so it did.

I still cannot believe that it has been twenty years since I last saw Elisabeth Schwarzkopf, whom I first met in 1981, the year my father published *On and Off the Record*, acquired and brilliantly edited by his colleague Marshall De Bruhl—her memoir and collection of writings by her recently deceased husband, Walter Legge, the legendary record producer at EMI and arguably the past century's most influential impresario in classical music.

I had escorted her around a maze of publishers at the Frankfurt Book Fair that fall and later, as my reward, attended her master classes over the next three years at the Mannes College of Music in my hometown, New York. Fifteen years later, in 2000, we renewed a friendship via phone and fax, prompted by my arranging for a reissue of the book, for which I had the enviable assignment of choosing photographs from her collection, composing her captions in the first person (the ultimate reward for an accidental life in publishing), and thereby retracing vicariously her luminous career.

This morning, as she greeted me at her door, two decades vanished in an *Augenblick*: Her face shines with expression, her eyes sparkle with wit and warmth, and her voice rings as clear in speech as on record. She directs me into her music room, awash in pale winter light. Though February is still a day away, we are surrounded by flowers in full bloom, a collage of color photographs she took of the gardens her husband planted for her over the years, to welcome her home from world-ranging tours of concert and opera stages. We are seated on an eighteenth-century loveseat for most of our first two-hour session; on a delicate table in front of us, beside my recording equipment, is a tray of coffee and sweets; I cannot help thinking of *Der Rosenkavalier*, Act One, *sans* libretto.

"Don't you want any cream?"

"No thanks—tell me when to stop," I reply, adding a touch to her cup (recalling that Hemingway used to request from my dad "just enough to change the color").

"More cream, please—it is not yet forbidden."

Dominating the room is a grand piano, closed, but with a vocal score on top; at the side, by the picture window, a brass music stand displays a framed photograph of Legge; another, still larger portrait of her late husband hangs on the far wall, directly facing—appraising?—the would-be pianist.

I confessed to Elisabeth my early obsession with Mozart; as a boy pianist I could readily identify with Schroeder in *Peanuts*, except that the bust on my piano was of Wolfgang, not Ludwig. I used to commute back and forth from piano bench to phonograph, to listen and then try to imitate Walter Gieseking playing the simplest minuets (on classic recordings of all Mozart's piano music collected aptly on Angel Records and produced by—who else?—her husband, Walter Legge).

"At least they seemed simple," she interjected. "Ah, Gieseking! Do you know that when he accompanied me on that record of Mozart lieder, he never used the pedal once? That was really something unheard of—and it was perfect."

The mention of the first pianist I ever heard had struck a welcome chord.

"We do have to learn not to sing like the piano," she continued, "which is not a legato instrument—and it is very difficult because it is the instrument that most singers hear accompanying them. Pianists use the pedal to make it seem legato, but Gieseking didn't: He didn't touch the pedal at all; he just played and it sounded legato."

Were there other accompanists she recalled as fondly? "Sawallisch was a wonderful accompanist; he accompanied my very first recital in London, and was hardly known at all—and I was not known—and we made it with that first recital in London. Sawallisch was much underestimated in his knowledge of what music is about. It is not glittering: It is about finding the right sounds at the right moment, at the right length, at the right strength, and finding that the sound fits the meaning of what Mozart meant in accompanying the words."

I was still thinking of Wolfgang the child prodigy and his family life in Salzburg. I asked what she thought about the possibility of a musical gene running through families.

"Not gene," she insisted. "I'd rather use the word 'instinct.'"

I asked about her parents; which of them passed on that instinct to her?

"My father took his guitar with him when he went off to fight in the First World War. He was very musical and he made me learn the guitar immediately."

Then, all of a sudden, we were back to time present: "Why did you travel so far to see me? I can't give you a performance."

"You give me a performance every day through your recordings."

"I haven't listened to a single record in this room for three years—I started one, but the acoustics were so wrong that I finished it in two minutes and never heard another. All the CDs I have heard are a terror, not the right sound, you know; and we have lived for the sound, *lived* for the sound—and that sound was not to take us to the heights of heaven but to bring out the composer's work in the best possible manner.

"I am not a musicologist, but I can tell you what I hate most now: people who dare to put Mozart into a different time. I find it such a crime to put Mozart visually into a different time, to make people who never knew of him like him and come and hear him because he looks more like themselves. This is the utmost crime against music. I left the Salzburg theater [in 2002] after the first act of *Don Giovanni*, you know. These producers are nearly criminal."

I was already aware of how important visualization has been in Schwarzkopf's artistry—she often called herself an "*Augenmensch*" (visual person)—

which has long fascinated me as an art historian. When coaching Bach's *St. Matthew Passion*, for instance, she would have a student picture the famous crucifixion by Grünewald. She delighted especially in the landscapes of Monet—those "visible blessings of the past," as she once described them to me. But visualization was not only an internal process in crafting hues of color and light. The scene has to fit the notes.

"It has to be in the time which Mozart wanted us to see it," she insists. "At Salzburg, we had the most wonderful producers with the deepest respect for Mozart."

Had she seen a change since then?

"Have I seen it! I didn't have to do it, thank God. I wouldn't have done it. In my time it went on with perfect visual representation. Our great conductors would never have allowed otherwise. Today it's all about money, money, money—all in modern costumes or none! The public should be educated—they should not be coming to see naked girls, but to listen to Mozart."

Is Mozart ideal training for young singers? Can young singers perhaps harm themselves by singing too much Mozart too soon? Here she was far more reassuring.

"No, Mozart is the ideal schooling for singers—but in the style of Mozart, not of Verdi or Wagner. The fixed style of Mozartean singing has rules, things you must do and things you must on no account do."

It comes as no surprise to a Schwarzkopf fan that her touchstone is *legato*, that quality of seamless singing in which she is peerless,

"You don't learn it through the piano, but through stringed instruments. I played the viola—

not very well, but at least I had to play it. The ear is your most important instrument in making music; the ear will tell you, 'Well, that wasn't legato, that note was finished too soon, why don't I bind it, why can't I sing it in one strength out, why don't I sing as it is written in a diminuendo and then go pianissimo to the next note, legato, or sing it with a crescendo and go to a legato even in a *subito piano* after a crescendo?' All those things have to be learned via the ear, your own ear.

"Likewise, the singer has to put the right person into the sound—not your person, but the person that Mozart wanted to hear. It shouldn't just sound like Miss Schwarzkopf! The Cherubino voice is different from the Susanna voice—they are all different—and you have to have so many different voices in your voice if possible—and it is not always possible—so they may still recognize me as Schwarzkopf but they should also recognize today, 'Aha, that is Susanna!' or the next day, 'Aha, that is the Countess!'—the same opera, but different ways of singing.

"This is what you have to learn in the *Hochschule* or with a teacher or with your own *Fantasie*, your own imagination. Imagination is the means of translating into your singing a feeling of what art is and what a great composer is. You cannot sing one piece like the next."

Throughout her career she deliberately limited her roles—in some, she said, "the sound was not right for me," and in singing "you must do justice to the persona in Mozart's cast." One role that fit like a glove, a velvet one at that, was the Countess in *Figaro*. She remains, for me, the definitive Contessa.

"It was Furtwängler who most influenced me, with the sound, with the expression you must feel the second before the note. When you talk, you alter your expression every second, every part of a second; you should do that when you sing."

"So, then, no matter how carefully crafted a performance, there is always the element of the almost instantaneous?"

"Certainly."

The recording I have listened to more times than I can count, ever since I studied it for a term as a college student, is the Giulini *Figaro*, recorded after she had been singing the Countess for more than a decade. It was that conductor's first recording of a Mozart opera for Legge at EMI.

"Walter believed in him very much; I liked him very much. We all know he fought great battles inside himself to make it right, you see, to find the expression; you could feel it—that he was giving his utmost to do the right thing and never felt safe that it was the right sound; he battled for it all the time, and that brings forth great expression from a human being."

Hence the visceral excitement of a recording that has never staled in its infinite variety over decades of listening.

Speaking of battles, what about *Don Giovanni*? I had read recently that whenever Schwarzkopf sang another of her signature roles the opera might as well have been re-titled *Donna Elvira*! "Elvira is the most dramatic role you can do—though Donna Anna needs a bigger voice." Did she ever sing Donna Anna?

"The arias, yes, but not the role—no, I was really formed for Donna Elvira, I believe, because I did find—I did feel—the right expression."

But Schwarzkopf's Elvira was so magnetic, so attractive—how could the Don have ever ditched her? She once tried to fight nature and make herself repulsive.

"I put on a false nose and face and made her a very cruel-looking person but it didn't work at all. Besides, if you cannot make the vocal character clear to the audience without showing her, there would be no phonograph records."

My favorite photograph from the archives, on the other hand, is a masterpiece of *chiaroscuro*—her blond Elvira opposite Leontyne Price's Donna Anna at Salzburg; my confession evoked a smile of happy memory.

"Ah, her voice was unusually beautiful, she had great expression—it's a totally different voice from mine, totally different character—and very, very good singing; there was not a flaw, never any kind of thinking back to singing Verdi or Puccini; she sang pure Mozart. She had the brains and the taste of a great artist. It was stylistically perfect. She knew exactly what you must never do in singing Mozart, what you should always have in your ear when you sing the note."

To what should this be credited, I wondered?

"Talent, number one. Instinct, number two. Then training is utmost." What of cultural background?

"Irrelevant. I have a young Japanese singer here who sings with utmost stylistic perfection already."

So does she actually think that our European heritage will move eastward?

"Absolutely. They learn so fast—the Japanese, Chinese, and Korean singers—the minute you tell them something, they do it. It is quite incredible. I have never experienced anything like it. And the tradition will pass from Europe to these other countries."

I couldn't repress a certain wistfulness, Eurocentric that I am. Schwarzkopf, however, has no such qualms.

"Not at all—because the tradition will *live*!"

Is it because there they are more respectful of our tradition?

"Not only more respectful, but talented! They have the will—and the understanding—to produce the right sound, and not just the sound but the feeling."

I reminisced about my first trip to the Frankfurt Book Fair and Wiesbaden, where I attended a performance of *Così* in a truly cozy house, an ideal intimate staging. "I did *Don Giovanni* there," Elisabeth recalled with special warmth. She had helped settle her parents in that delightful eighteenth-century spa town for their twilight years.

Is Mozart, then, better suited to smaller houses?

"Yes, of course, because the discussion—the recitative—in Mozart is very fast, and passes by so quickly, and is so important for details of expression; it gets lost in a huge space."

By contrast, she explained, *Der Rosenkavalier* was composed to fit a large opera house, and the dialogue moves more slowly; but not so in Mozart. "The houses are too big these days; some are even filled with microphones—it's a bloody sin!"

Whom of her colleagues would she single out as great Mozart singers? "Karl Schmitt-Walter, the baritone—he could really sing Don Giovanni, and lieder, and God knows what." The best of them combined opera with lieder, she said. I asked about my pirate CD of the Salzburg *Figaro* she performed with Dietrich Fischer-Dieskau. Was he as good on stage as in recital?

"Yes, because of how he sang the role; there was not one phrase, not one note that was not perfectly performed from breathing in and breathing out. He completely matched—in movements, expressions—what he sang: a great actor as well as singer, which is not always the case. The acting must never be overdone but must always underline the singing—*prima la voce!*"

And what of Christa Ludwig (a favorite Octavian for vicarious pursuit of my Marschallin)?

"This is one of the best voices we have ever had, you know, a very full voice, very musical; she could be serious or funny or whatever; she could do everything. We were really comrades on the stage; she always reacted as one hoped she would react. And she was a marvelous concert artist— she had it all."

How then did Schwarzkopf come to learn a Viennese style of singing Mozart?

"Well, I had two years of singing in Vienna's Theater an der Wien. Many of the roles I had to learn overnight, so I really learned the Vienna style of singing in those two years. But I also had a year out in the sanitarium in the Tatra Mountains of Slovakia, recovering from tuberculosis, and I took all my music with me and spent that year lying in the woods memorizing all the parts I wanted to sing—not singing, just memorizing."

Not every singer, I ventured, would make such an investment from such a setback.

"I think it was pure instinct."

Her teacher, Maria Ivogün, had helped make the arrangements; across the room her smiling picture faced us atop the bookshelf, flanked by two deep cobalt vases. I had mistaken the photo of Ivogün for young Elisabeth: Beauty plays such tricks.

"Karl Schmitt-Walter took me to her when I was a beginner at the Berlin Opera. I was already two years at the opera house, but Maria told me I had no technique, and we started with two notes; for four months we did nothing but those two notes, and then slowly we went up bit by bit, for two years."

What about Ivogün's husband, pianist Michael Raucheisen, with whom Schwarzkopf performed her first lieder recitals?

"He was the most wonderful accompanist in all the world, the greatest accompanist that ever was—*punto, finito.*"

I wanted to turn the clock back even further— to the earliest years of study; we had both attended all-boys schools—an ocean and era apart. Hers was due to the fact that her father was headmaster. There she learned to play a host of instruments, from the lute and *Glockenspiel*, to the organ (though her feet could not reach the pedals), and she sang the role of Mary in Christmas pageants.

Years later, progressing through Mozart roles at the Deutsche Oper, she began with Blondchen in *Die Entführung*, and then Konstanze. In *Die Zauberflöte* she started in the chorus—for the famous Beecham recording produced by her future husband, Walter Legge, in 1937—then sang one of the three boys, and finally Pamina.

"I could never sing Queen of the Night; I could not have done the F; I was not a coloratura. It was really foolish to have sung the E [in *Entführung*] because if you don't have the reserve on top you should never do it."

But she did, thank God—and recordings have preserved its purity for half a century. In *Figaro*, she passed through Barbarina to Susanna and finally the Countess, the role she owned for the rest of her career.

Which Mozart role remained the most dramatically and vocally challenging?

"Even the slightest folksong is challenging all the time. But I would have to say Fiordiligi, which is very long and very hard to sing well. You have to hold a true position of your voice throughout, and you really don't even have a minute to go to your dressing room!"

I had recently been to a rehearsal of the Met's *Così*, which is more traditional and tasteful than so many European counterparts ("Thank God for that!"), and I wanted to know whether she had ever experienced the novel—dare I say perverse?—couple-swapping at the new ending that had so unsettled me. She had not.

"It would make no sense, since all is forgiven. It's just a director wanting to call attention to himself." She calls such modern liberties "crimes—or foolishness—against Mozart."

Nor does Mozart permit wide vocal liberties, she added—no surprise that he was not a favorite of Callas or so many Italian singers who thrive on a free range.

"The one thing in Mozart is control. Woe to you as a singer if you don't fit into the conductor's picture of sound, speed, loudness, softness, expression . . . there are about three hundred things that go into style. An artist must act respectfully toward the composer, just as the composer showed respect for the text."

I thought back to another photo I had selected for her book. What about her early Don in Salzburg, Tito Gobbi?

"A great Don Giovanni—ideal. Although being Italian he could sing Mozart. He sang perfectly. It isn't easy for an Italian to give up the freedoms that are not allowed in Mozart."

What about Nicolai Gedda, to shift to tenors?
"Ideal."

Moving still farther north, I reminisced about the Swedish conductor Sixten Ehrling, who had once studied with Strauss and shortly before he died gave me his vocal score of *Der Rosenkavalier*. I now imagined it placed on top of this Marschallin's piano, right in front of us. Did she ever accompany her students on the piano?

"Yes, sometimes. I had a Japanese student who came here for a day and stayed three weeks. For teaching Mozart I could accompany her to give her the right ideas—technical ideas, not musical ones. Musical ideas you can work out only with a very good pianist."

It was now time to pretend—in the spirit of Walter Mitty—that I was her student. "What is the most important thing for a student of Mozart?"

"The timbre of the voice, the sound of the voice—it has to be an utterly beautiful sound, and not just the notes as such. That sound will vary from the *secco* recitatives, to the accompanied ones, to the first notes at the beginning of the aria, which is again not quite the sound of the aria itself, and so on."

After all the preparation, can a singer allow herself at the moment of singing an aria to enjoy the emotion, of joy, sorrow, whatever, that is being conveyed to the audience?

"No, you must be able to put your feeling into the sound and to hear what you are doing; the ear is all important."

What of the current vogue of spontaneity, of just being yourself?

"No, because there is the matter of style, and the style is in the music—and if Mozart hasn't got style I don't know who has—and that style needs observation, it needs knowledge, it needs hearing, what you are doing wrong, a feeling for the tempo, for changing of color, as permitted: You don't have a lot of freedom in Mozart, but you don't have to be afraid of giving beauty to Mozart if it is true to style . . . and you must always obey the conductor, because Mozart is not conducted by nitwits!"

The theologian Karl Barth once quipped that in heaven Bach was court composer but that every afternoon the angels sneaked off to play Mozart. I wanted to know Elisabeth's appraisal of that court composer, since I have long been addicted to her early recordings of his cantatas, spun with a young voice of pure silver.

Bach, she replied, is "fiendishly difficult to sing—I'd rather five times Mozart than one-half time Bach!"

Then I asked the question to which I was convinced I already had the answer: What composer, if she were allowed only one, would she keep for herself?

"Smetana."

I should know better than to second-guess Schwarzkopf. Why Smetana? His "richly loving folk sound," she replied. Not so much the vocal music as his orchestral music. Her father had loved Smetana, and so did she. Even with no roots in Czech soil, she found listening to that composer "always a kind of homecoming."

I was determined to salvage Mozart. Surely he was the most gifted, the most ingenious of composers?

"I don't know. I think he is the most feared to do justice to, because not doing so is immediately audible, immediately exposed."

Why? Isn't Bach technically as difficult?

"More difficult, but Bach does not touch you in the same way as Mozart does. Mozart is so simple, touching you immediately with just a few notes. Bach needs many more notes to touch you."

After Dame Elisabeth enumerated the grueling details of traveling, packing, unpacking, doctors, and everything that precedes performing on tour, I asked her to pretend I was now her agent and asking her preference: a staged opera, opera in concert, or a recording?

She recalled fondly those concert performances of Mozart operas arranged by her husband in London's Festival Hall.

"You don't act across the stage but you do react to each other. I think those are the ideal performances because you don't have to concentrate on whether that chair will break down, or whether I have the right dress, but can concentrate on singing. Those were the very best opera concerts I ever did."

I was surprised to hear this from someone as gifted in acting as in singing.

"But, you know, you can still act while standing still. You can look and listen and react to what your partners are singing. More is not needed. In the recording studio, on the other hand, one does not have the freedom even to turn and look to the side but must stand completely still and focus on the score."

I asked her to list the great Mozart conductors she sang under. "Furtwängler, number one; Krips, Sawallisch, Böhm, Giulini. He was never happy with his performance, you know, but he was marvelous."

What about Klemperer, whom her husband had put in charge of the Philharmonia Orchestra?

"He was very slow—too slow—but when you were singing with him you believed him; he was very respected."

At two o'clock—or was it closer to three?—it was clearly time for a break, and Elisabeth encouraged me to go to the top of the Hochjoch for a late lunch and for a loftier view from the mountains she has loved all her life. So I rode up on a car. Everyone else had skis; I had my camera. I have been deathly afraid of heights all my life, but today there was no turning back. I hope the film develops; the views were breathtaking.

When I took the cable car back down I suddenly saw that I was returning to late-afternoon shadow after the snow-reflecting sunlight of just minutes earlier. I'd never realized how much illumination mountains steal from the valley between them. No wonder Moses—and prophets to follow—sought and found God on a mountaintop. *Lux umbra Dei*: "Light is the Shadow of God."

Yet more revelations lay below. Elisabeth's eyes had been bothering her today, and when I arrived at six in the evening she suggested that I postpone our conversation until tomorrow. But I was determined not to leave as soon as I'd arrived, and so I pointedly left all the recorders in the bag and offered to do something practical for her, explaining that I have been well trained by both my mother and my wife.

She had me open a bottle of red wine for her—a "glass and a half"—and as I sipped water we talked over a range of subjects, starting with religion (prompted by her framed photo of our mutual friend Cardinal Schönborn of Vienna). Elisabeth said she is a great admirer of Cardinal Schönborn, whom I ventured may someday be pope. She beamed as she declared, "He is very courageous; he says what he thinks." (Obviously a kindred soul.)

To her protests that she considered herself "neither Protestant nor Catholic" and "hardly pious," I countered that St. Augustine once said that "whoever sings prays twice." Her singing has surely given more glory to the Creator than a lifetime kneeling in church.

We talked of Strauss's librettist Hugo von Hofmannsthal, whom she considers a great poet.

"Everything one needs to know about life, about living life, is in *Der Rosenkavalier*"—words of wisdom by the ultimate Marschallin of our age. ("*Ja, ja.*")

Elisabeth then turned to the framed photograph of her beloved father, "Poppi," and told me of his lifelong love of books and how his treasured library had been saved in Berlin and shipped to storage in Bavaria toward the end of the war by devoted soldiers who had served under him on the Russian front. The middle-aged classics teacher had been conscripted to identify the fallen, notify their families back home, and make the arrangements for burial.

By the end of our two-hour talk on and off the record, I asked whether I might go into the music room and play her piano alone—to see whether I might have the nerve to play for her tomorrow.

She said yes, but added she would not promise not to follow me!

And so she did. Sitting by my side, she stopped me measure by measure, and offered the most insightful critique and piano lesson I have ever experienced. I should have practiced days if not weeks before coming here. What was I thinking? I sat and waited for the obvious conclusion: "No wonder you are a writer."

Instead she looked at me with clear blue eyes of wonder and asked, "Why are you not performing?"

To all my excuses—that it was a childhood pursuit, that I didn't have the talent, that it was too late, that I didn't practice—she countered, "But you must play. Why do you want to write about music when you can make it? You have time to perform—do it!"

I hedged. I would love to have been able to sing, I said.

"But that is not your instrument. The piano is. Make it sing—and thank God it exists."

Before I flew over here I wrote to one of my sons that at the risk of sounding morbid I felt that I was going to Schruns "to meet my fate." I was jesting in earnest. But now it is no joke: Life will never be the same. I shall go back to practice, back to musical scores, back to the keyboard of my childhood. Down deep I have always suspected that my musical laziness has taken a toll in true satisfaction, if not happiness. But it took a Dame of the British Empire and a *Kammersängerin* to put it into words—and with blunt, incredulous honesty. Our interview tomorrow will be interesting, to say the least. And I have already promised to return and play again—but after real practice.

Wednesday, February 1, 2006

I hardly slept at all last night. Was it the cream sauce on the pasta I had for dinner—or something even less easily digested? The realization that a new route has been pointed out for me and life will never be the same again? I cannot afford to procrastinate or rationalize. Elisabeth speaks with nine decades of experience and a life offered on the altar of music.

As she remarked, music is the only "saint" or holy art permitted in nearly every church of every denomination, from Catholic to the most iconoclastic Protestant. I shall no longer have the luxury of protesting that I am out of practice—that is no longer an option. As my late dad put it, "No rush, just do it immediately."

This morning's visit to Elisabeth at eleven was far more relaxed, but it was clear from the start that I would never get her to philosophize about singing or even Mozart's characters. I heard, in the mind's ear, the echo of her Marschallin gently scolding her beloved Octavian in the early morning light: *"Philosophier' Er nicht, Herr Schatz!"*

She was no philosopher, she protested to me, but "purely practical," and her secrets were reserved only for other singers—of which I am not one. She discounts journalists and critics; hence her conviction that I should exchange my laptop keyboard for a holier one—that of the piano!

But then I explained, as I unpacked the recorders, that I was no critic, nor was I a journalist. In fact, this was my very first interview. She was startled: Why did you come all this way then? As a pilgrim, I replied—to give thanks to the singer who illuminates my every week, if not day, via recordings. I came purely as a lover of her singing and of Mozart—a listener who still buys her vinyls on eBay to savor the original sound—not as a professional journalist or critic. This interview, I explained, was an afterthought with *Opera News*.

"Be sure to tell your readers," she instructed—and so I do.

We moved into the music room and I switched on the recorders for another two hours of discussion . . . What about the recent revival of lesser-known Mozart not performed in her day? *Idomeneo* and *Tito*?

A good thing, she said, but unfortunately a temptation to producers to "put their hands on the piece to make it more popular."

I made the mistake of describing my young son Charlie's first experience of *Don Giovanni* on television some fifteen years ago, via Peter Sellars and set in Spanish Harlem, complete with a McDonald's takeout for the Don's feast.

"Why was he allowed that? Totally idiotic—not only idiotic but a crime, a crime against Mozart."

She didn't want to hear about Sellars' *Così* set in a roadside diner.

"Please don't poison my memories!"

Among the fonder memories of recent years are those of her former pupil Thomas Hampson, whose "sound is utterly beautiful." And the mention of Anna Moffo, her maid Susanna in the Giulini *Figaro*, evoked the same adjectives: "An utterly beautiful voice—and she was intelligent in addition, which is not always the case, you know."

The definitive Susanna? "Irmgard Seefried, to whom everybody else must be compared—and that isn't easy!"

I wanted to learn more about what she termed the "Mozart sound." Even though he wrote Italian operas, it is not an Italian sound, she explained. The Mozart sound remains constant, whether in German or Italian. So how does a young singer find it?

"They have to be taught. You know, sometimes I make students sing a sound thirty times and suddenly on the thirty-first time: 'Ah, that is the sound you are supposed to make.'"

How did she herself find it? Through her teacher Maria Ivogün, and Michael Raucheisen, and later her husband, Walter Legge.

"He had a phenomenal ear and a phenomenal idea of music, not only of Mozart but of all music."

Would she envision the sound in terms of other instruments?

"Not at all—it is enough to have to know your own instrument!"

Yet she would study the full orchestral scores when preparing a role. Violins are key, for they alone can "imitate the vibrato of the human voice." For instance, when singing a passage in which the first violins take the second voice, in accompaniment as though a duet, "you listen to that violin and try to make your voice as similar as you can to that vibrato."

To me, Schwarzkopf made opera singing sound like a chamber music ensemble.

"But of course it is—do you think it could be otherwise? You need to listen closely to the orchestra, to the solo instruments, because the mood of the aria is already set in the introduction which offers the most revealing notes about the aria, because the aria is but the feeling of what you have said about the situation in the recitative."

So studying the recitative is no minor matter?

"Oh, no—it is more important than the aria!"

It was time to approach, gingerly, the heart of the matter: Why is Mozart the most widely beloved composer? Why not Haydn or Handel, who wrote so many more operas to choose from?

In three words, "*His melodic instinct*—non-musicians can leave whistling his melodies."

Schwarzkopf is unusual among singers for her fidelity and devotion to the written texts of the librettists as the inspiration and illumination of the composer's notes. Last night, speaking of Hofmannsthal, whom she considers a great poet, she told me that "everything you need to know about living life is in *Der Rosenkavalier*." So much for the singer who had earlier protested that she had nothing philosophical to say, only the most practical things about the craft of singing!

She remains ever my Marschallin. What opera of Mozart's comes closest to that appraisal of Hofmannsthal?

"*Figaro*, of course."

What then does she make of *Die Zauberflöte*?

"It's like a fairy tale, and it should not be in any way seriously meant in terms of punishments and so on . . . no, no—it is a fairy tale about people who want to do the best with their lives and can't."

What about productions that put the emphasis on Masonic mysteries?

"No, no—it's very simple; simple expressions and moments—of being loved, of not being loved—in everybody's life. It is a mistake to make it too philosophical because the music is not philosophical at all; the simpler it is presented, the more pity you have for Pamina."

She enjoyed those early years of singing that role: "Pamina was not at all difficult." Again, she stressed the need to keep it simple, "not like a folk song— it's a different simplicity, and we all know how difficult it is to be simple. Sometimes you have to have a lot of life behind you in order to be simple. If I give you very simple answers it is not because I have only lived five minutes, you know."

We took a break as Elisabeth rose from the loveseat to take a turn around the room. I offered to try to get her turntable turning again, and to play for her the record of *Messiah* highlights, produced by her husband in 1964, his last year at EMI, which I had bought on eBay and brought over to add to her collection.

Her hi-fi was more complicated than any system I have ever confronted, and the large framed photo of Walter Legge did not increase my confidence. But finally I got it to work.

Her arias "Rejoice, greatly" and (my own favorite) "I know that my Redeemer liveth" gave her no cause for rejoicing: Elisabeth was merciless in her self-critique ("not legato . . . okay, that's my sound . . . no, that's flat . . . I don't think I like it . . . but it is a clean intonation").

More frustrating was the fact that the system amplified the extremes at the expense of the middle range, which seemed to her (not to me) to disappear.

I was hopeless as in-house technician, but I forged ahead and suggested we listen to "Porgi amor" from the Giulini *Figaro*, my Mozartean grail.

It took me awhile to find it, as the record in her library was the Japanese edition ("not legato . . . good . . . *ja* . . . ok . . . no . . . there are things that are really not perfect").

Would it be interesting, I asked, to hear the same aria recorded ten years earlier? "Yes . . . cruel, cruel but interesting . . ." I protested that it's surely never cruel to get younger. "Well, I hope it is better."

I put on the 1950 Vienna recording with Seefried and Jurinac. She was at this point moving from years of Susanna to the Countess; did she still hear the voice of Susanna?

"Yes, all of it . . . marvelous piano . . . it's very clean, but it's a child's voice . . . very sweet . . . because of the cleanliness you have to uncover the E, you know . . . but it's a child's voice . . . it's ideally clean but not ideal for the Countess." For intonation she preferred this recording, but its sound was not "ripe enough for the Countess, much too young."

When I protested that both the Countess and she were indeed young (she was only thirty-four, the Countess perhaps a few years younger), she quipped, "Well, I wasn't eighteen, you know." The Countess is wiser, and should sound "riper," she concluded.

So I moved on to play Strauss's "*Die heiligen drei Könige*" and then Mozart's "*Ridente la calma*," with Gieseking, which I found enchanting; but Elisabeth herself heard Italian that sounded too German and a clean voice "that could be any soprano's." She considered her "ideal" voice that of the Marschallin; I could hardly disagree. But a Brahms duet with Fischer-Dieskau wore out my welcome with the machinery. "I think you'd better put that

energy into piano playing," she said, laughing.

So I retreated to the piano for a second impromptu coaching session before leaving for the airport. I felt it only fair that I put myself on the receiving end of criticism after inflicting so much audible pain through the poorly tuned loudspeakers.

I started with a Bach prelude in C-sharp; the piano itself was sharp, her criticism even sharper—and to the point.

"Could you make it sound like a discussion between the hands? Softer there . . . discussing . . . two people discussing, all the time . . . come in with the left hand . . . give me those four bars piano . . . *ta-ta*, quick . . . two people fighting, discussing."

Then on to Beethoven's "Ecossaises."

"Take an audible breath . . . can you make that an echo . . . make that less beautiful . . . *more!*"

I reminded her that I had taken six trains to reach her; I would not turn back now. Her final prescription was to add more *Fantasie* to the pieces once the technique had been secured. The Haydn sonata, for instance, needed "more visible humor, wit"; the repeats, more color, more variety. The Scarlatti should be turned into a conversation among as many as four people.

Finally, the Chopin "L'adieu Waltz."

"Can that seem more like a viola coming in there? Start again . . . Ah! Left hand . . . you need more freedom . . . you are not thinking of singing, and you should . . . even breathing, in and out."

It is not just about the notes, she stressed.

"There are so many possibilities in the music: It's about adding the feelings and human reactions."

I asked whether her performances, even after years of preparation, might change.

"Absolutely, always, in a moment."

She suggested I study some comic actors for the range of human reactions to be translated through the keyboard. Opera without words, or *Lieder ohne Worte*.

"You should be able to work the piano music into a human expression."

It is, in the end, all a matter of *Fantasie*, her favorite word, of our imagination; not a matter of technical precision—that is just the skeleton (which of course must be sound) on which the flesh-and-blood interpretation makes a piece of music a living thing.

"Music without thoughts, without ideas," she said, "is a waste of time." She claims to be no philosopher, just a "practical singer"—she doth protest too much.

Little did I know what I would take away from this visit, which was initially intended not as an interview but a thank-you for all those years of grace and vocal paradise via recordings. We opened a copy of the new edition of *On and Off the Record,* the homage to Walter Legge.

My favorite photo is one of her looking upward, like a Guido Reni saint in ecstasy—not singing but "listening" (as she inscribed on the verso—"*Hören!*"). And that, I concluded, was the key to her success and to her vocal embodiment of the glory of Mozart, *da capo al fine*.

As we said *auf Wiedersehen*—not good-bye—and I promised to practice her lessons before returning in summertime with my wife, Ritchie, she told me to waste no time getting to the keyboard. But which keyboard? Her final question, an encore from last night, gave the answer: "Why do you want to write about music when you can make it?"

Thursday, February 2, 2006

I went home by another route. I explained to Elisabeth that I would gladly take six trains to see her, but not to leave her. And I promised to return with Ritchie and with some proof that I had returned for good to the piano. Her driver took me to Zürich airport, and I was able to get to Paris a day early—or rather, a late night early.

I stayed at a splendid hotel without ever leaving the Air France terminal, before boarding my early morning flight to New York. The Sheraton is designed like a ship, with beautifully appointed wood cabins. If a real ocean liner could replicate this experience—with some added rocking and salt air—I might yet be lured onto a cruise.

These pilgrimages are exhausting; I may need a week to recover. But even for someone who loathes leaving his zip code, it was well worth it. For so many years I have cast Elisabeth in the role of my musical standard and conscience. This visit confirmed the choice. It could not have been better.

Toward the end of the visit, as I crossed the music room to come around to the other side of the loveseat, she turned to me and said, "You know, in this light you seem about seventeen years old!" Then after a pause, she added, "Perhaps part of you still is?" *Ja, ja.* I always loved being a student; it is too late to give it up.

Postscript: Portions of this pilgrimage journal were published in the July 2006 issue of *Opera News* under the title "The Voice of Mozart." I sent Elisabeth a copy, and held my breath until a phone call from her a week later. She told me that of all the profiles written of her over the years, this one was her favorite, and despite her long-standing aversion to digital recordings of any kind, she graciously gave me permission to have her 1963 Canadian broadcast of *A Viennese Evening,* a television special with conductor Willi Boskovsky, issued at last for the public on DVD (now available from VAI).

She had once lamented to me, *auf Deutsch,* that her voice "had been sacrificed on the altar of CD convenience and commerce" (my translation) and she much preferred the warm sound of the original analog vinyls produced by her late husband and still available via eBay, thank God.

But her enduring affection for that Viennese evening with Maestro Boskovsky overrode any ingrained technical reservations. She recalled that recital with such fondness that her voice, suddenly sounding decades younger over the transatlantic phone line, resonated with delight. That was the last time I spoke with her; two weeks later, on August 3, she died in her sleep.

How I wish I could have revisited her before the end of summer, as originally planned. But I now treasure all the more that *Wienerabend* DVD as her parting gift to us all—a foretaste of heaven.

"Die Zeit, die ist ein sonderbar Ding . . . auch sie ist ein Geschöpf des Vaters der uns alle erschaffen hat." *("Time is a strange thing . . . yet it too is a creation of the Father who made us all.")*

In Memoriam: Elisabeth Legge-Schwarzkopf (1915–2006)

Selected Discography

This selection features major recordings available on CD and DVD. For the most complete discography and informed discussion of Schwarzkopf's recording career, still being supplemented by pirated and posthumous releases, the reader is directed to Alan Sanders and J. B. Steane's *Elisabeth Schwarzkopf: A Career on Record* (Amadeus Press, 1996).

Johann Sebastian Bach

St. Matthew Passion. 1961. Peter Pears, Dietrich Fischer-Dieskau, Elisabeth Schwarzkopf, Christa Ludwig, Nicolai Gedda, Walter Berry. Philharmonia Orchestra of London, conducted by Otto Klemperer. EMI Classics.

Mass in B minor. Historic recording in mono. 1952. Elisabeth Schwarzkopf, Marga Höffgen, Nicolai Gedda, Heinz Rehfuss. Philharmonia Orchestra of London, conducted by Herbert von Karajan. EMI Classics.

Ludwig van Beethoven

Fidelio. Live recording, Covent Garden. 1947. Hilde Konetzni, Elisabeth Schwarzkopf, Paul Schöffler, Ludwig Weber, Peter Klein, Karl Friedrich. Covent Garden Orchestra, London, conducted by Clemens Krauss. Istituto Discografico Italiano.

Symphony No. 9. 1951. Elisabeth Schwarzkopf, Elisabeth Höngen, Hans Hopf, Otto Edelmann. Chorus and Orchestra of the Bayreuth Festival, conducted by Wilhelm Furtwängler. EMI Classics (Great Recordings of the Century).

Johannes Brahms

Deutsche Volkslieder (German Folksongs), nos. 1–42. 1965. Elisabeth Schwarzkopf and Dietrich Fischer-Dieskau, with Gerald Moore. EMI Classics.

Ein deutsches Requiem (A German Requiem).
a) Historic recording. 1947. Elisabeth Schwarzkopf, Hans Hotter. Vienna Philharmonic, Wiener Singverein, conducted by Herbert von Karajan. EMI Classics.
b) 1961. Elisabeth Schwarzkopf, Dietrich Fischer-Dieskau. Philharmonia Orchestra and Chorus (London), conducted by Otto Klemperer. EMI Classics.
c) Live recording, Lucerne. 1947. Elisabeth Schwarzkopf, Hans Hotter. Lucerne Festival Orchestra and Choir, conducted by Wilhelm Furtwängler. Music & Arts.

Engelbert Humperdinck

Hansel and Gretel. Complete recording. 1953. Elisabeth Schwarzkopf, Elisabeth Grümmer, Else Schürhoff, Maria von Ilosvay, Anny Felbermayer, Josef Metternich. Philharmonia Orchestra of London and the Bankcroft's School Choir, conducted by Herbert von Karajan. EMI Classics.

Franz Léhar

Das Land des Lächelns (The Land of Smiles). Complete recording. 1953. Double CD with *Die lustige Witwe (The Merry Widow).* Elisabeth Schwarzkopf, Emmy Loose, Nicolai Gedda, Josef Schmidinger, Otakar Kraus, Erich Kunz, Anton Niessner, *et al.* Philharmonia Orchestra of London, conducted by Otto Ackermann. EMI Classics.

Die lustige Witwe (The Merry Widow). Complete recording. 1962. Elisabeth Schwarzkopf, Hanny Steffek, Franz Böheim, Eberhard Wächter, Josef Knapp, Nicolai Gedda, Kurz Equiluz , *et al*. Philharmonia Chorus and Orchester, conducted by Lovro von Matačić. EMI Classics.

Gustav Mahler

Symphony No. 2, "Resurrection." 1962. Elisabeth Schwarzkopf, Hilde Rössl-Majdan. Philharmonia Chorus and Orchestra, conducted by Otto Klemperer. EMI Classics (Great Recordings of the Century).

Des Knaben Wunderhorn (The Youth's Magic Horn). 1968. Dietrich Fischer-Dieskau, Elisabeth Schwarzkopf. London Symphony Orchestra, conducted by George Szell. EMI Classics.

Symphony No. 4 and Lieder. 1961. Elisabeth Schwarzkopf, Christa Ludwig. Philharmonia Orchestra of London, conducted by Otto Klemperer. EMI Classics.

Wolfgang Amadeus Mozart

Cosi fan tutte.
a) 1954 (in Italian). Elisabeth Schwarzkopf, Nan Merriman, Lisa Otto, Léopold Simoneau, Rolando Panerai, Sesto Bruscantini. Chorus and Philharmonia Orchestra of London, conducted by Herbert von Karajan. EMI Classics.
b) Complete recording. 1962 (in Italian). Elisabeth Schwarzkopf, Christa Ludwig, Hanny Steffek, Alfredo Kraus, Giuseppe Taddei, Walter Berry. Philharmonia Orchestra and Chorus of London, conducted by Karl Böhm. EMI Classics.

Die Zauberflöte (The Magic Flute). Abridged recording (no recitatives). 1964.
Agnes Giebel, Gundula Janowitz, Lucia Popp, Ruth-Margret Pütz, Anna Reynolds, Elisabeth Schwarzkopf, Marga Höffgen, Nicolai Gedda, Karl Liebl, Gerhard Unger, Walter Berry, Gottlob Frick, *et al*. Philharmonia Orchestra and Chorus, conducted by Otto Klemperer. EMI Classics.

Don Giovanni.
a) Complete recording. 1959 (in Italian). Joan Sutherland, Elisabeth Schwarzkopf, Graziella Sciutti, Eberhard Wächter, Piero Cappuccilli, Luigi Alva, Gottlob Frick, Giuseppe Taddei. Philharmonia Orchestra and Chorus of London, conducted by Carlo Maria Giulini. EMI Classics.
b) Live recording, Salzburg Festival. 1954 (in Italian). Elisabeth Grümmer, Elisabeth Schwarzkopf, Erna Berger, Cesare Siepi, Otto Edelmann, Anton Dermota, Walter Berry, Ernster Dezsö. Vienna Philharmonic, conducted by Wilhelm Furtwängler. EMI Classics.

Le Nozze di Figaro (The Marriage of Figaro).
a) Historic recording, in mono. 1950. Elisabeth Schwarzkopf, Irmgard Seefried, Sena Jurinac, Elisabeth Höngen, George London, Erich Kunz, Erich Majkut, Wilhelm Felden, *et al*. Vienna Philharmonic and Vienna State Opera Chorus, conducted by Herbert von Karajan. EMI Classics
b) Live recording, Salzburg Festival. 1957. Elisabeth Schwarzkopf, Irmgard Seefried, Christa Ludwig, Sieglinde Wagner, Dietrich Fischer-Dieskau, Erich Kunz, Alois Pernerstorfer, *et al*. Vienna Philharmonic and Vienna State Opera Chorus, conducted by Karl Böhm. Orfeo.

c) Complete recording, in stereo. 1959. Elisabeth Schwarzkopf, Anna Moffo, Giuseppe Taddei, Eberhard Wächter, *et al.* Philharmonia Orchestra, conducted by Carlo Maria Giulini. EMI Classics.

16 Lieder and Quintet for Piano and Wind Instruments, K. 452, in mono and stereo. 1956. Elisabeth Schwarzkopf, Walter Gieseking, Philharmonia Wind Ensemble. EMI Classics.

Lieder and Concert Arias. 1955 and 1968. Elisabeth Schwarzkopf, with Walter Gieseking and Alfred Brendel. London Symphony Orchestra, conducted by George Szell. EMI Classics.

Opera Arias (from *Don Giovanni, Die Entführung aus dem Serail, Le Nozze di Figaro, Idomeneo,* and *Die Zauberflöte*). 1946–52. Elisabeth Schwarzkopf, various orchestras and conductors. EMI Classics.

Jacques Offenbach
Les Contes d'Hoffmann (Tales of Hoffmann). Complete recording (in French). 1964. Nicolai Gedda, Elisabeth Schwarzkopf, Victoria de los Angeles, Gianna d'Angelo, Nicola Ghiuselev, George London, Ernest Blanc, *et al.* Orchestre de la Conservatoire, Paris, conducted by André Cluytens. EMI Classics.

Carl Orff
Die Kluge. Complete recording (together with *Der Mond*). 1956. Elisabeth Schwarzkopf, Rudolf Christ, Paul Kuen, Marcel Cordes, Benno Kusche, Hermann Prey, Gottlob Frick, *et al.* Philharmonia Orchestra, conducted by Wolfgang Sawallisch. EMI Classics.

Giacomo Puccini
Turandot. Complete recording. 1957. Maria Callas, Elisabeth Schwarzkopf, Eugenio Fernandi, Nicola Zaccaria, Giulio Mauri, *et al.* Orchestra and Chorus of La Scala, Milan, conducted by Tullio Serafin. EMI Classics.

Franz Schubert
24 Lieder. Historic recordings, 1948–65. Elisabeth Schwarzkopf, with Gerald Moore and Geoffrey Parsons. EMI Classics.

Lieder and Piano Pieces. 1952. Elisabeth Schwarzkopf, Edwin Fischer. EMI Classics.

Richard Strauss
Vier letzte Lieder (Four Last Songs) and 12 Orchestral Lieder. 1965. Elisabeth Schwarzkopf. Berlin Radio Symphony Orchestra and London Symphony Orchestra, conducted by George Szell. EMI Classics.

Arabella. Highlights. 1954. Elisabeth Schwarzkopf, Nicolai Gedda, Josef Metternich, *et al.* Philharmonia Orchestra of London, conducted by Lovro von Matačić. EMI Classics.

Ariadne auf Naxos. Complete recording. 1954. Elisabeth Schwarzkopf, Rita Streich, Irmgard Seefried, Rudolf Schock, Hermann Prey, *et al.* Philharmonia Orchestra, conducted by Herbert von Karajan. EMI Classics.

Capriccio. Complete recording. 1957. Elisabeth Schwarzkopf, Christa Ludwig, Anna Moffo, Eberhard Wächter, Dietrich Fischer-Dieskau, Nicolai Gedda, Hans Hotter, *et al.* Philharmonia Orchestra, conducted by Wolfgang Sawallisch. EMI Classics.

Der Rosenkavalier. Complete recording. 1956. Elisabeth Schwarzkopf, Christa Ludwig, Teresa Stich-Randall, Otto Edelmann, Eberhard Wächter, *et al.* Philharmonia Orchestra and Chorus conducted by Herbert von Karajan. EMI Classics.

Arabella (Scenes)/*Capriccio* (Final Scene)/*Four Last Songs.*1953–54. Elisabeth Schwarzkopf, Josef Metternich, Murray Dickie, Walter Berry, *et al.* Philharmonia Orchestra of London, conducted by Lovro von Matačić. EMI Classics.

Four Last Songs, Orchestral Songs, and *Finale from Act I* of *Der Rosenkavalier.* 1961 and 1965. Elisabeth Schwarzkopf, Radio Symphony Orchestra of Berlin and London Symphony Orchestra, conducted by George Szell, together with Hertha Töpper (soprano) and the Philharmonia Orchestra of London, conducted by Charles Mackerras. EMI Classics (CD and DVD).

Johann Strauss
Die Fledermaus. Complete recording. 1955. Rita Streich, Elisabeth Schwarzkopf, Nicolai Gedda, Erich Kunz, Rudolf Christ, Helmut Krebs, Karl Dönch, *et al.* Philharmonia Orchestra and Chorus, conducted by Herbert von Karajan. EMI Classics.

Giuseppe Verdi
Falstaff. Complete recording. 1957. Anna Moffo, Elisabeth Schwarzkopf, Nan Merriman, Fedora Barbieri, Tito Gobbi, Luigi Alva, Rolando Panerai, Renato Ercolani, *et al.* Philharmonia Orchestra and Chorus, conducted by Herbert von Karajan. EMI Classics.

Requiem and *Four Sacred Pieces.* 1962–64. Elisabeth Schwarzkopf, Christa Ludwig, Janet Baker, Nicolai Gedda, Nicolai Ghiaurov, *et al.* Philharmonia Orchestra and Chorus, conducted by Carlo Maria Giulini. EMI Classics.

Hugo Wolf
Italian Songbook. 1965. Elisabeth Schwarzkopf, Dietrich Fischer-Dieskau, Gerald Moore. EMI Classics.

Italian Songbook / Mörike and *Goethe Lieder.* 1956–65. Elisabeth Schwarzkopf with Gerald Moore. EMI Classics.

Spanish Songbook, Nos. 1–44. 1966. Elisabeth Schwarzkopf and Dietrich Fischer-Dieskau, with Gerald Moore. Deutsche Grammophon.

Collections

A Tribute to Gerald Moore. 1967. Works by Mozart, Schubert, Brahms, Hugo Wolf, *et al.* Elisabeth Schwarzkopf, Victoria de los Angeles, Dietrich Fischer-Dieskau, Gerald Moore, Daniel Barenboim, Jacqueline du Pré, *et al.* EMI Classics.

Unpublished Recordings, 1946–1952. Works by Arne, Bach, Gounod, Morley, Mozart, Puccini,

Schubert, Strauss, Verdi, and Wolf. Elisabeth Schwarzkopf, Gerald Moore, Jean Pougnet, Norman Feasey, Philharmonia Orchestra, Vienna Philharmonic, conducted by Walter Susskind and Josef Krips. Testament.

The Unpublished EMI Recordings, 1955–1958. Works by Bach and Mozart. Elisabeth Schwarzkopf. Philharmonia Orchestra of London, conducted by Otto Ackermann and Thurston Dart. Testament.

The Unpublished EMI Recordings 1955–1964. Works by Bizet, Brahms, Mozart, Schubert, Schumann, Strauss, Wagner, and Wolf. Elisabeth Schwarzkopf, Gerald Moore, Walter Gieseking. Testament.

Elisabeth Schwarzkopf 1915–2006. Works by Bach, Gluck, Humperdinck, Mahler, Mozart, Puccini, Schubert, Schumann, J. Strauss, R. Strauss, Verdi, Wolf. Elisabeth Schwarzkopf, Elisabeth Grümmer, Kathleen Ferrier, Karl Schmitt-Walter, Walter Gieseking, Gerald Moore, Geoffrey Parsons. Philharmonia Orchestra of London; Orchestra and Chorus of La Scala, Milan; and the Vienna Philharmonic, conducted by Thurston Dart, Wilhelm Furtwängler, Josef Krips, and Herbert von Karajan. EMI Classics.

For My Friends. Farewell recording. 1977 and 1979. Works by Brahms, Grieg, Loewe, Wolf. Elisabeth Schwarzkopf, with Geoffrey Parsons. Decca.

Great Moments of Elisabeth Schwarzkopf. 1946–59. Works by Bach, Bizet, Dowland, Handel, Humperdinck, Mozart, Puccini, Schubert, Schumann, Smetana, R. Strauss, Verdi, Wagner, Weber, Wolf. Elisabeth Schwarzkopf, Margreta Elkins, Irmgard Seefried, Teresa Stich-Randall, Christa Ludwig, Gerald Moore, Karl Hudez. Various orchestras and conductors. EMI Classics.

Operetta Arias. 1957. Works by Heuberger, Lehár, Millöcker, J. Strauss, Suppé, Zeller. Elisabeth Schwarzkopf. Philharmonia Orchestra conducted by Otto Ackermann. EMI Classics.

Elisabeth Schwarzkopf Sings Richard Strauss. Recordings of 1965 and 1968. *Lieder*, op. 10, 27, 36, 37, 41, 43, 48, 49, 56, and 88, and *Four Last Songs*. Elisabeth Schwarzkopf. Philharmonia Orchestra, Radio Symphony Orchestra of Berlin, conducted by George Szell. EMI Classics.

Elisabeth Schwarzkopf Sings Wolf. 1953. Selected *Lieder*. Elisabeth Schwarzkopf, with Wilhelm Furtwängler (piano). EMI Classics.

Elisabeth Schwarzkopf and Irmgard Seefried Sing Duets. 1947–55. Works by Carissimi, Dvorak, Humperdinck, Monteverdi, and Strauss. Elisabeth Schwarzkopf, Irmgard Seefried, Gerald Moore, Philharmonia Orchestra of London and Vienna Philharmonic, conducted by Josef Krips. EMI Classics.

Songs You Love. 1957 and 1966. Lieder by Brahms, Grieg, Martini, Mozart, Schubert, Schumann, Sibelius, R. Strauss, Wolf, *et. al.* Elisabeth Schwarzkopf with Gerald Moore. EMI Classics.

The Very Best of Elisabeth Schwarzkopf. 1950–67. Works by Bach, Beethoven, Heuberger, Humperdinck, Lehár, Mozart, Schubert, Sieczynski, Smetana, J. Strauss, R. Strauss, Volksgut, Wagner, Weber, and Wolf. Elisabeth Schwarzkopf, Elisabeth Grümmer, Josef Metternich, Gerald Moore, Walter Gieseking, Edwin Fischer, Harold Jackson. Various orchestras and conductors. EMI Classics.

Elisabeth Schwarzkopf Sings Operetta. 1957. Selections from operettas by Heuberger, Lehár, J. Strauss Millöcker, Suppé, Zeller. EMI Classics.

Operetta Arias. Historic recordings of 1939–40 and 1953. Works by Lehár, J. Strauss, Suppé. Elisabeth Schwarzkopf, Nicolai Gedda, Rupert Glawitsch, Josef Schmidinger, Otakar Kraus, Erich Kunz. Philharmonia Orchestra of London, Chorus and Orchestra of the Deutsche Oper Berlin, conducted by Hans Georg Otto and Lutze Walter. Hänssler.

DVDs

Elisabeth Schwarzkopf: A Viennese Evening (Une soirée viennoise), with Willi Boskovsky. Radio Canada. 1963. Operetta selections by Suppé, J. Strauss, Heuberger, Zeller, Lehár, and Sieczynski. Telecast of October 31, 1963. Elisabeth Schwarz-kopf. Orchestre de Radio-Canada, conducted by Willi Boskovsky. With memorial booklet by Charles Scribner III. VAI.

Elisabeth Schwarzkopf: A Self-Portrait. 1995. EMI Classics.

Richard Strauss. *Der Rosenkavalier.* Complete recording and staged production from the Salzburg Festival, 1960. Available in the UK and Europe only. Elisabeth Schwarzkopf, Sena Jurinac, Anneliese Rothenberger, Otto Edelmann, Erich Kunz, *et al.* Vienna Philharmonic and Chorus of the Vienna State Opera, conducted by Herbert von Karajan. Director: Paul Czinner. BMG RCA Red Seal.

Richard Strauss. *Legend. Four Last Songs, Orchestral Songs* and *Finale of Act I of Der Rosenkavalier.* 1961 and 1965. Elisabeth Schwarzkopf and the Radio Symphony Orchestra of Berlin and London Symphony Orchestra, conducted by George Szell, together with Hertha Töpper (soprano) and the Philharmonia Orchestra of London, conducted by Charles Mackerras. EMI Classics (CD and DVD).

Schwarzkopf, Seefried, Fischer-Dieskau: Gustav Mahler, *Songs of a Wayfarer;* Richard Strauss, *Lieder* and selections from *Der Rosenkavalier.* 1961. Elisabeth Schwarzkopf, Irmgard Seefried, Dietrich Fischer-Dieskau. EMI Classics.

Acknowledgments

Kirsten Liese

These days, high-quality illustrated books about great singers or musicians are a luxury. Television and film stars with audiences of millions can be marketed far more easily. Thus it became clear that a book worthy of Schwarzkopf, one of the greatest singers of the last century, would need a sponsor. But where to find one at a time when large renowned organizations such as the Berliner Filmfestspiele must find a new sponsor to replace one that has fallen by the wayside?

Elisabeth Schwarzkopf indirectly led me to Annemarie Schindler, who became our generous patron, as she was waxing lyrical about her on the telephone and invited me to her first master class at the Villa Schindler in Tirol: "Frau Schindler is a wonderful entrepreneur who supports young talent and who battles against the cultural decline so apparent in opera today. Sometimes you just want to run away from what you see and hear. Such a commitment is not to be taken for granted. It is a rare thing when people are prepared to invest in culture. She is setting a superb example."

It was no coincidence that Elisabeth Schwarzkopf held her last two public master classes at the Villa Schindler in April 2005 and June 2006, where she felt truly at home. She enjoyed the ambience within the small circle of connoisseurs. Annemarie Schindler had previously worked another small wonder in October 2004 when she arranged at her villa a joyful reunion between Elisabeth Schwarzkopf and the Italian pianist Aldo Ciccolini (p. 128).

Annemarie Schindler is a great admirer of Elisabeth Schwarzkopf and they had an affectionate bond. Frau Schindler alone was allowed the privilege to film and photograph the ninety-year-old while she was teaching. Thus it became a labor of love to compose as a memorial to the distinguished Mozart and Strauss singer this illustrated book, for which I deeply thank Annemarie Schindler with those apt words that Elisabeth Schwarzkopf herself wrote to her in a letter of June 2006: "For one year you have been an essential part of my life. I have never known another lady who dedicates her life in this way to the promotion of art, and I hope that you will continue to take on such projects in the future."

I am particularly grateful to the Villa Schindler and the Salzburg Festival for their generous support. Further thanks go to the Bayreuth Festival, the Deutsche Oper Berlin, the Bayerische Staatsoper, EMI Classics, the Teatro alla Scala, the Deutsche Kinemathek Berlin, the Friedrich-Wilhelm-Murnau Foundation, and the Bundesfilmarchiv (Federal Film Archive).

The following people have been at my side, assisting with both words and deeds: Gudrun Eckle, Claire Erlanger, Monika Faltermeier, Lillian Fayer, Ulla Fröhling, Dr. Geerd Heinsen, Margret Kothe, Renate and Wolfgang Liese, Dr. Guntram Lins, Carola Ott, Thomas Rakow, Charles Scribner, Adelheid Söns, Annemarie Schindler, Jacqueline Schwarz, Swantje Steinbrink, Susannah Worth, and Ute Ziemer.

Furthermore, I would like to thank the following people for writing contributions especially for this book: Aldo Ciccolini, Claire Erlanger, Dietrich Fischer-Dieskau, Brigitte Fassbaender, Mirella Freni, Elisabeth Furtwängler, Thomas Hampson, Renate Holm, Christa Ludwig, and Wolfgang Sawallisch.

Charles Scribner III

As translation editor, I should like to thank especially Dr. Barbara Strawitz of Baton Rouge, Elisabeth Schwarzkopf's devoted friend for over four decades, who provided constant encouragement, suggestions, corrections, warmth, and wisdom throughout this labor of love and memory.

Claire Erlanger, as dear and indispensable to Elisabeth as she had been to Walter Legge, first put me in touch with the author, Kirsten Liese, and thus initiated our year-long adventure in music, art, and collaboration, for which I am most grateful.

My fellow opera lovers Kathryn and Corbin Miller, whose impeccable musical taste is rivaled only by their gift of friendship, offered invaluable support and guidance.

Marshall De Bruhl, my late father's longtime publishing colleague and friend, first signed up for Scribners and then brilliantly edited Elisabeth's book *On and Off the Record*; it was he who introduced me to the most glorious and pitch-perfect author on record, or stage, ever published by our family. A generation later, now an eminent historian and author, he generously gave me the benefit of his peerless editing and—a true "editor's editor" whom Schwarzkopf herself gratefully admired—he left no page of my Epilogue unimproved. John Cerullo, publisher of the aptly named Amadeus Press, embraced the idea of an English-language edition of this beautiful photo-biography and has given it an international afterlife worthy of its subject. *Vielen Dank!* Finally, special thanks are owed—and gratefully acknowledged—to Carol Flannery and Clare Cerullo at Amadeus for producing a book as beautiful as its subject.

Index of Names

Photo Credits

Archiv der Bayreuther Festspiele 36 (below)
Archiv Deutsche Kinemathek Berlin 18, 27
Archiv der Salzburger Festspiele 55, 71, 73 (Anny Madner); 48, 49, 50, 51, 57, 58, 59, 60, 61, 62, 72, 92, 93, 108 (Karl Ellinger); 28 (Max Reinhardt Archiv)
Andreas Barylli 12
Beth Bergman 111
Jerry Darvin 42
Deutsches Münchner Theatermuseum / Archiv 26 (Willy Saeger)
Zoe Dominic 94
EMI Classics 115, 116
Claire Erlanger 118, 122, 123 (above), 135
Milla Escobar 112
Lillian Fayer 14, 32, 33, 34, 35 (above), 38, 46, 47, 53, 54, 64, 65, 66, 68, 69, 70, 76, 81, 84, 85, 87, 90, 97, 98, 102, 103, 104, 105, 106, 110, 113 (below)
Friedrich-Wilhelm-Murnau-Stiftung 24, 25
Getty Images 99

Norman Gryspeerdt 91
Maria José Más Marqués 77
Gérard Neuvecelle 128 (above)
Privatarchiv Elisabeth Schwarzkopf 22, 23, 30, 39, 40, 41, 43, 44, 63, 67, 74, 75, 78, 79, 80, 107, 113 (above), 114, 119, 120, 121, 123 (below), 124, 125, 126, 127, 129, 130, 134 (Collection Zumikon)
Helga Sharland 36 (above)
Annemarie Schindler 128 (below)
Theatermuseum der Mailänder Scala 37, 52 (Erio Piccagliani)
Victoria and Albert Museum London 82, 83, 88 (Houston Rogers)
Bruno Völkel 29

In some individual cases the owners of the photograph reproduction rights could not be traced. The publishing house requests that any existing requirements be communicated directly with them.